1381

Penguin Books
The Country Railway

3964
(3)

Eve
Dav
in 7
the
an e
beer
Boo
trav
jour
196(
of v

David St John Thomas

The Country Railway

Penguin Books

Penguin Books Ltd, Harmondsworth,
Middlesex, England
Penguin Books, 625 Madison Avenue,
New York, New York 10022, U.S.A.
Penguin Books Australia Ltd, Ringwood,
Victoria, Australia
Penguin Books Canada Ltd, 2801 John Street,
Markham, Ontario, Canada L3R 1B4
Penguin Books (N.Z.) Ltd, 182–190 Wairau Road,
Auckland 10, New Zealand

First published by David & Charles 1976

Published in Penguin Books 1979

Copyright © David St John Thomas, 1976

Made and printed in Great Britain by
Butler & Tanner Ltd, Frome and London
Set in Monophoto Ehrhardt

Contents

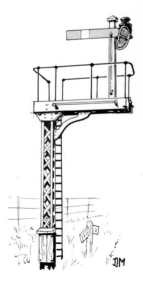

THE ILLUSTRATIONS

Illustrations not acknowledged in the captions and not from the author's collection or that of Locomotive & General Railway Photographs are: British Railways, 10, 11, 23 top, 38 top, 39, 165; R. H. Darlaston, 8, 123 bottom; Stephen Bartlett, 40, 83; Roger Sellick, 46, 108, 111, 131; E. E. Smith, 47; John Goss, 48, 58, 94, 167, 168, 172–3, 178; Peter Gray, 50–51, 60 top, 123 top; H. C. Casserley, 57, 60 middle and bottom, 134 middle; G. D. King, 69, 98 bottom, 117, 159 top; Geoffrey Kichenside, 79; P. J. Fowler, 84; M. C. Kemp, 85, 112, 113; John Thomas, 87 bottom; M. Montgomery, 90–91; J. S. Hancock, 98 top; C. R. L. Coles, 102; Ivo Peters, 103 top; Donald R. Barber, 103 bottom; P. B. Whitehouse, 128, 151 bottom; W. H. Austen Collection, 133; E. C. Griffith, 136; P. Ransome-Wallis, 141, 144; E. M. Patterson, 151 top; Loco Publishing Co., 159 bottom; Stanley Creer, 174; Geoffrey N. Wright, 175 top; Yorkshire Dales National Park, 175 bottom; Yorkshire County Trust 178. Also see acknowledgements on page 186.

1 Introduction

Platform, refreshment room, approach road milled with onlookers, most casual, some intent. Cameras flashed as a party of boys in top hats laid a wreath on the locomotive, and a sandwich-board mockingly declared that 'The End Is At Hand'. Enthusiasts gathered round the guard to persuade him to let them board the five coaches standing at the platform. 'It's advertised as an empty train and if you get on it won't be empty'; irrefutable. Reluctantly they stood back and the crowd sang 'Auld Lang Syne' as the engine exploded detonators and the train disappeared lamely into the night. Nobody hurried to leave; people talked of the old days, of when everyone came and went by train, of father telling how he had helped build the line, of how uncle had lost money on it, of grandson aged seven who had taken his very first train trip that afternoon. The refreshment room was packed and noisy, given an extension licence to celebrate its own demise.

The date was 3 November 1962; the place Helston, market town and capital of Cornwall's Lizard peninsula. After a fierce battle in which local dignitaries had complained that the facts and figures on which British Railways had based their case for closure were incorrect – an allegation which British Railways chose to ignore – the last passenger train had run with many a moist eye and practical as well as sentimental regret. From Monday anyone coming from London could no longer change from the *Cornish Riviera Express* straight into a waiting branch train at Gwinear Road; many local residents would have to buy cars or change jobs.

It was a typical branch-line funeral, locals as well as enthusiasts from far and wide making sure that their railway should at least have a decent burial which would itself become folklore. The muddles behind it were also typical. British Railways had undoubtedly presented wrong information to the Transport Users' Consultative Committee which had to assess how much hardship the closure would cause; but even so, the passenger service clearly lost money heavily and buses could carry the traffic – if only they had been less unimaginatively arranged. That final train was itself a comedy of errors: normally the last train of the day was stabled at the terminus, but knowing that tonight it must return to the main line, people had asked permission to sign off the service by riding it. Twice district headquarters at Plymouth had denied it would return; it did of course, empty because no official, not even a railway policeman, turned up to represent the management, and the good-natured crowd, though bitter with the indifference of railway officials, were unwilling to get the one harassed guard into trouble.

This was just before Dr Beeching, appointed head of British Railways to bring them into the twentieth century, published his report proposing massive use of the axe. Other closures were indeed in abeyance pending the report's appearance. Like many other lines at this time, Helston lost only its passenger trains, the daily freight continuing, an intermediate signalbox remaining to cope with the two trains that would use the line simultaneously during the Cornish broccoli season. So the route duly continued losing money until its total closure five years later.

Helston station shortly before closure.

One of the Great Western's early buses.

It never paid, but without it Helston and the Lizard area would have been less prosperous, the horticultural industry and tourism would not have expanded. The district had indeed suffered by being left off the railway network until late in history. The line which self-effacingly hugged the contour across the undulating plateau was built by the money and effort of local businessmen in 1887; they could no longer stomach having to pay more for fertilizers and the coal to heat their greenhouses than their competitors near main-line stations such as Marazion and Penzance. Helston once had the solid assurance of Penzance, but had slipped behind in the two decades that trains had linked its rival to the thrust and opportunities of national life; even its streets were not properly lit, a new gasworks being built beside the station as soon as it opened. Two years later the Great Western absorbed the local railway company – at a considerable discount on its capital cost. The local businessmen had achieved their purpose. Helston's economy was revitalized. Plans to extend the line to the Lizard might have gone forward had not the motor bus appeared.

9

The Great Western chose this route for the first of its many bus services; in 1903 the 22-seater was welcomed to the roads it was frequently to churn up.

The closure of the Helston branch has been chosen for our starting point, but another could have been picked from a score or more in south-west England alone, each line having character, built by local enterprise to ensure that some little part of the country received its coal and fertilizers as cheaply as possible, that the mail arrived promptly, that beer did not cost more than in neighbouring places, and above all that local industries and crops could compete fairly in a wider market. For to

Farm removals were once a common feature on country railways, the farmer and his family, tractor and car, live and dead stock, travelling by a special train that had to stop occasionally to water and feed the animals and even milk cows. The vehicles in the picture below are part of a farm-removal train from a Welsh to a Surrey village in 1927; the picture on the facing page shows part of another farm removal 10 years earlier.

despatch cattle to the nearest railhead ten miles away might cost as much as sending them 100 miles by train – and upcountry buyers were reluctant to come to fairs not reached by train and where arrangements generally were backward.

In most areas for at least two full generations all important comings and goings were by train. The price of coal nearly always fell by a third with the opening of the local line, and every new piece of agricultural machinery also came on the freight. Calves, day-old chicks, pigs and other reinforcements for the local livestock normally came by passenger train along with the mails, newspapers and local soldiers on leave. The pair of rails disappearing over the horizon stood for progress, disaster, the major changes in life: the route to Covent Garden and Ypres, the way one's fiancé paid his first visit to one's parents, one's children returned for deathbed leavetaking, the way summer visitors, touring theatricals, cattle buyers, inspectors came. Even when most people made local journeys by road, the railway retained its importance for the long,

HELSTON and GWINEAR ROAD.—Great Western.

Up.		gov	mrn	aft	aft	gov	gov
Helston	dep	9 40	1125	1 48	4 35	6 40	7 48
Nancegollan		9 51	1140	1 59	4 46	6 51	7 59
Praze		9 57	1150	2 5	4 52	6 57	8 5
Gwinear Rd. 19, 18	arr	10 5	12 0	2 13	5 0	7 5	8 13
Penzance 18	arr	1044	1243	3 50	5 25	....	8 46
Plymouth 19	"	1 50	....	6 47	7 55	1025	....

Millbay Station,		gov	mrn	mrn	aft	aft	1&2
Plymouth 18	dep	6 50	9 20	11 0	2 35	....	6
Penzance 19	"	16 0	....	2 5	....	6 35	gc v
Gwinear Road	dep	1057	1230	2 45	6 7	7 15	8 38
Praze		1045	1 1	2 53	6 15	7 23	8 46
Nancegollan		1051	1 10	2 59	6 21	7 29	8 52
Helston	arr	11 2	1 21	3 10	6 32	7 40	9 3

GWINEAR ROAD and HELSTON (1st and 3rd class).—Great Western.

Miles	Down.				Week Days.							Sundays.		Miles	Up.				Week Days.							Sundays.	
		mrn	mrn	aft	aft	m	aft	aft			mrn	aft				mrn	mrn	mrn	mrn	aft	aft	m	aft	aft	mrn	aft
	Gwinear Road	dep	7 10	8 55	1040	1245	3 15	4 50	5 20	6 55	9 20	..	7 10	5 35	..		Helston	dep	6 30	7 55	9 50	1155	1 55	4 10	5 55	6 20	8 35	..	5 45	4 10
2¾	Praze		7 18	9 2	1047	1252	3 22	4 58	5 28	7 2	9 28	..	r	r	..	1½	Truthall Platform	..	3 0	..	12 0	..	4 15	..	6 27	8 40	..	r	r
5	Nancegollan		7 24	9 8	1054	1259	3 29.5	4 5	3 34	7 9	9 34	..	7 50	6 15	..	3½	Nancegollan		6 41	8 10	1 12	8 2	5 4	23 6	6 6	34 8	48	..	6 11	4 36
7	Truthall Platform		..	9 16	..	1 6	..	..	5 40	7 15	..	..	..	..	..	6	Praze		27	6 47	8 14	10 7	21 4	2 12	4 29	6 12	6 40	8 54	..	..
8½	Helston	arr	7 35	9 24	11 5	1 14	3 40.5	13 5	5 48	7 22	9 45	..	8 20	6 45	..	8½	Gwinear Road	22	6 55	8 22	1015	1 22	2 21	4 38	6 20	6 48	9 2	..	6 55	5 20

m Motor Car, one class only. **r** By Road Motor.

ǁ Station for Porthleven (2¾ miles), Mullion (6 miles), The Lizard (10 miles), Kynance Cove (10 miles), Housel Bay (10½ miles),
Cadgwith (9¼ miles), and Coverack and St. Keverne (10¼ miles).

The Lizard.—Road Motors leave Helston Station at 7 45 and 11 15 mrn., and 5 25 aft. for the Lizard.
Cars also leave the Lizard at 8 20 mrn., 2 45 and 4 15 aft. for Helston Station.

The basic service of 1887 (gov stands for government or trains carrying passengers at the one-old-penny-per-mile rate Gladstone introduced in Parliament; sometimes 'parl' was used instead) was substantially increased by 1910 when the railway used its pioneer buses not only to extend business to the Lizard but to give Helston main-line connections on Sundays.

vital if occasional trips to the rest of the world, and Helston is only one of the towns less easy to reach from London now.

But the country railway provided more than transport. It was always part of the district it served, with its own natural history, its own legends and folklore, a staff who were at the heart of village affairs, its stations and adjoining pubs places for exchange of gossip, news and advice. Its mourners recognized that more than British Railways' statistics showed would be lost when it died.

2 The Building of the Branch Line

One of the wonders of history is the speed with which Britain's railways were built, changing with their creative destruction life patterns in town and country alike. Almost everywhere the main system was finished by 1860, a mere thirty years since Stephenson's Liverpool & Manchester first carried passengers quicker than the speed of an animal. The most important English towns left without trains even in 1854 were Hereford, Yeovil and Weymouth, though Wales and Scotland were then sparsely served. With the trains came prompt national newspaper deliveries, mass-produced foodstuffs, fertilizers and building materials, the fast movement of perishable commodities, standard Greenwich or 'railway' time, and by no means least the electric telegraph, at first exclusively a railway appendage. In thirty years the Britain we know today had been firmly established, the coming of the railways coinciding with – and directly advancing – a rising social conscience and political reform. Sewerage systems and gas lighting appeared in at least half of England's country towns during this period – as citizens became more aware of what was necessary; the great holiday resorts took shape, and agriculture crept forward. The newspapers of 1860 have more in common with those of today than the small, tightly-packed libellous sheets which a generation earlier so often saw the triumph of Stephenson's *Rocket* as an item of far less interest than the current local scandal.

With curious exceptions, the trunk lines were naturally the first to be built; their promoters were keen to link the big centres of population, but ready enough to supplement traffic through intermediate stations serving market and other towns of any size. The character of the country station was already firmly established in 1840. Some of the trunk routes also threw out short stubs to serve places a few miles off – perhaps to towns like Eton which originally refused to be placed on the main line,

Part of one of the famous Bourne plates portraying the making of Tring cutting on the London & Birmingham Railway in 1831, the year after the opening of the Liverpool & Manchester. The straightest and most level lines were generally those built first.

quickly regretted it, and never recovered. And then the process of infilling began. With such enthusiasm did Britain take to the railways that by the early 1840s it seemed commercially suicidal to be left running a business in an area without trains. Line followed line as armies of navvies moved around the country. There might be 2,000 men and 300 horses employed tipping some 2,500 wagons a day, each containing $2\frac{1}{2}$ cubic yards of earth, for a single embankment, or the same number of men split between half a dozen gangs over a line eight miles long; 500 men could be concentrated on building a single bridge or over 1,000 on a longish tunnel, often working in shifts round the clock, tearing through hills and filling in valleys to create a moderately level route for the new Universal Mover.

Speculation of course culminated in the Railway Mania of 1845. In that year and the following two Parliamentary sessions, no fewer than 650 railway Acts were passed authorizing the construction of nearly 9,000 miles of track (today's total system is only 11,000 miles), much of it in deepest countryside. Many more applications were refused by Parliament at high cost to their promoters, only a few of whom tried again. Even some who obtained their Act found the cost far higher than expected and were unable to use the powers conferred. Just how expensive the initial stages could be is told by Peter Baughan in his history of one of Yorkshire's most rural lines, the Wharfedale Railway. In 1849 the directors told shareholders they should plan to begin construction. 'They were, in fact, whistling in the dark. By this time they had called up or loaned just over £65,000 and had spent nearly £46,000 between the company's formation on 20 January 1845 and 31 December 1848. The heaviest expense had been for legal and Parliamentary matters totalling £21,731

Making a cutting.

Another famous picture, from F. S. Williams' Our Iron Roads.

7s 10d to date. Engineering and surveying, and compensation, had taken £8,000 and £7,000 respectively. And not a foot of track had been laid.'

The Railway Mania bubble burst, and thereafter the story of railway building has a singularly familiar ring: credit squeeze, delays by bad weather, financial crisis, rising prices (as in the boom after the Franco-Prussian war), scarce money, unreliable advice and labour. Many of the lines started in the late 1840s (188,000 men were building 3,000 miles of uncompleted railways in May 1848) and early 1850s were not finished till years later; some not at all, an occasional useless cutting representing the life savings of local people. 1864 brought a particularly severe financial crisis.

Some branch lines and whole networks of branches were built by major companies, such as the North Eastern Railway, which from the start served its rural as well as industrial territory well, often laying in private sidings for individual farms. But most main-line companies had spent far more than expected on their trunk routes and were too committed to fill in the gaps themselves. So it was frequently left to local people to do so, as at Helston. Inspiration for a new line usually came from the furthest end: just as Bristol merchants had started the Great Western from London, so rural landlords and millowners threw their savings, their ingenuity, their lives, into connecting their district with the nearest main line. They might begin with a sense of obligation to ensure that their valley was not left out of the new steam scheme of affairs; often they had first tried in vain to persuade the main-line company to build the link. But all too often local patriotism became blind determination to present the case for the new route in the best possible light, minimizing physical and other obstacles, exaggerating traffic potential and social and economic benefits, conning people out of their savings.

The local papers of the 1840s and 1850s are packed with verbatim reports of public meetings to establish railway companies, a popular theme being that if the main-line company did not want to build the branch itself then local people must benefit from such short-sightedness. 'They should not go to London for an engineer. They considered there was talent enough in the neighbourhood for the construction of a line

A picture used to stir up opposition against a railway scheme; not even the sacred rural sport would be safe!

Perhaps Britain's most loved line is the West Highland which after crossing the wilds of Rannoch Moor, passing through a ravine on its descent into Fort William (where the train reverses) and then playing hide and seek with mountains, valleys and freshwater lochs, eventually passes beside the saltwater Lochailort with views out to sea and several of the Inner Hebrides shortly

before reaching that most romantic of termini at Mallaig. Here John Goss captures a Mallaig-bound train in the evening light in July 1974. The locomotive is No 27019. There is a double-page spread of other pictures of the West Highland on pages 172–3.

of 14 miles only' (Tavistock). Again, if they were not to be free of the main-line company (or the engineer, or any other railway company), 'he would have nothing to do with the scheme; for he thought they ought to be perfectly free for their own interest and the interest of the public'.

Prospectuses were concocted in glowing terms: 'Looking at the number of mills up the course of the line, the Factory and Brewery, and the number of Villages and Farms, it would run through or near, the goods traffic of corn, for grinding into flour, Hops and Barley for brewing, unmanufactured wool, Household and Steam coal, lime for building and agricultural purposes, Artificial manures, Slates, Tiles, Drain pipes, Bricks, Stone and Foreign timber, going up the line with Beer, Woollen Goods, Flour, Hay, Straw, English Timber, Meat, Butter and Cheese coming down the line, the traffic would be a fair one.'

Often there were rival schemes to connect the same places: Tories sometimes backed one line and Whigs the other. Friendships were made and broken. Joseph Thomas Treffry writes of a rival Cornish scheme: 'I hope my answer will be in time to save your friends money for a greater delusion has never been attempted in the whole history of Railways to be practised on the public than that contained in the prospectus in your favour of the 19th instant.' A week later – the year is 1844 – he writes to another friend who has told him he is wrong in the suspicion he is backing the rival: 'After being intimately known to each other and on friendly terms for nearly half a Century, the *report* of your canvassing for the other line grieved me exceedingly lest any representation should have been made to you without my having an opportunity of explanation.' But we later learn that the suspicion *had* been justified, for Treffry's line came too tight upon the other gentleman's property. Everyone wanted a railway, but not on his doorstep. Seldom a precise art in the hands of hastily-trained assistants, surveying often produced inaccurate information when done furtively at night or while the landowner's attention was distracted elsewhere. Once the route had been decided, it might have to be modified to avoid opposition, a tunnel, embankment or bridge even being built solely to preserve a short cut to hounds, or peace for the pheasants.

The obtaining of an Act was only the starting point, herculean task though it must have seemed to country people with no experience of Parliamentary proceedings and over-pressed agents. Raising the capital was the next: 'My dear Sir, As I am sure you would regret to find that the Cornwall Railway share list was filled without your name appearing on it, I hope you will excuse my troubling you to say that . . .'; and the London broker emphasizes the desirability of a stronger local representation among shareholders. Then again the consulting engineer finds the original route defective and wants to move it: 'By consent of the Landowner my Act empowers one to do so, and the saving of Land and the distance will be very great – All the resident parties are favourable to the Alteration, and if you will also have the kindness to consent to it the Railway through your land will be shortened by more than a mile.'

A plethora of comings and goings and excitements there must have been. Today, for all our experience of wholesale alteration of the countryside, we quail at the prospect of an electric pylon in our view; then, the exact *positioning* of the railway, leave alone its basic completion, must have given sleepless nights in villages and townships the length of the land. One captures something of the feeling in a minor country classic, *Small Talk at Wreyland*, reprinted several times in the 1920s. Cecil Torr quotes family correspondence to show that the first survey for a line from Newton Abbot to Moretonhampstead took place immediately after the arrival of the main line at Newton Abbot: 'They seem to be guided by the stream, and (if it takes place) they will go right up the meadows under here . . . I cannot fancy it will take place, for people are a little cooled down, and not so mad for speculation. Had it been projected some little time ago, no doubt it would have taken place.' That was in 1847 after the Mania had collapsed. Other surveys were abortive, but in 1856 perhaps the greatest of all the British railway contractors, Thomas Brassey, who employed thousands of men and undertook a vast range of schemes at home and abroad, appears on the scene. 'He is staying at Torquay for the benefit of his health, and rides over some part of it every fine day.'

Then on 17 November 1864, Cecil Torr's grandfather writes to his father: 'More than a hundred discharged on Monday, and a pretty row there was: drunk altogether, and fighting altogether, except one couple fought in the meadow for an hour and got badly served, I hear. The same night the villains stole all poor old xxxxx's fowls . . . there is not a fowl or egg to be got hereabouts.' Early next year he describes a visit from

Two contemporary (1840s and mid-1850s) views of the railway navvy.

a drunken navvy the day before: 'About as fine a built tall likely a fellow as you ever saw, and nicknamed the Bulldog. He asked for meat and drink, and was sent away empty. I learnt that he worked Saturday and Monday, and received 5s. 6d for the two days, slept in a barn and spent all his earnings at the public-house ... Not long after I saw the policeman who

Three groups of men on the job in the age of the camera. Top, building the Severn Bridge in the 1870s. Bottom left, widening part of the South Devon line at the turn of the century. Bottom, rebuilding Taunton station in 1895 – a station that was later to accommodate stopping country trains on seven different routes.

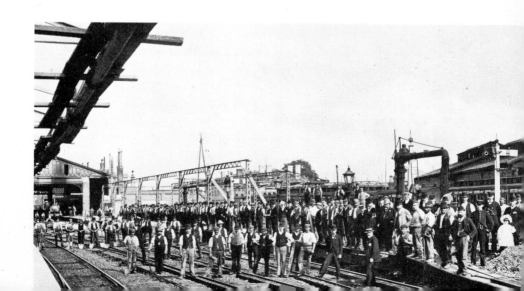

belongs to the line – not the Lustleigh man – and he said, "If anything of the kind occurs again, send for me, and I will soon put all right." But he spends all his time on the line keeping the navvies in order; and before he can be got mischief may be done.' One of the dogs was poisoned by meat thrown by a navvy; after that grandfather kept a revolver.

And so it was all over rural Britain. Navvies had a bad reputation, and that the hard-drinking hard-swearing Irish living rough in overcrowded huts upset the even tenor of any quiet English village is not hard to imagine. The villages that felt most terrorized were those near great tunnels and bridges where large numbers of navvies were camped for years on end. But one suspects that much of the inevitable general disturbance – the closing of roads, the mess and noise including that of the steam excavator used even on the Sabbath in later years, the luring away of farm labourers who could earn as much on the railway in three ten-hour days as all week on the land, the absence of pupils from school, the tearing apart of favourite coppices and fields, the putting up of food prices and occasional scarcities – has been too readily blamed on the navvy. (It was not much fun having a North Sea gas main laid down the lane the other year, and in our age disturbance is familiar and to be expected.) How could country people who seldom saw more than a handful of strangers in their valley not resent a mass invasion – and an invasion of men of a type they could not have met before?

Writing of the invasion in his Northamptonshire village at the turn of the century, S. J. Tyrell records in *A Countryman's Tale*: 'While the preliminary work was in progress, strangers were coming to the village in twos and threes, seeking accommodation. They were the contractors' regular men – engine drivers, foremen and skilled tradesmen. In those days most villages had empty cottages, but these were soon tenanted at what we thought exorbitant rents. A married man unable to find a cottage in one of the nearby villages became a lodger and kept an eye open for a cottage changing hands. Some of the poorer folk made a spare bedroom by squeezing the family together at bedtime, so that a lodger could be accommodated, glad of the extra shilling he brought into the house. The folk at the two Barnetts Hill cottages took in a surprising number of lodgers; they say the beds there never got cold when the steam navvy worked round the clock.' And it was only the contractors' select 'regular' men attempting to integrate with the village; the navvies kept apart in their own encampments. By this time the steam navvy (an excavator with continuous buckets) had reduced the number of hands required, and since there were then fewer railways to build some of the men stopped on in the village, revitalizing its life.

Of course there were riots and randies, deaths and maimings through drunkenness and temper or carelessness on the job; much that no decent countryman could have regarded as normal – the sleeping of twenty to thirty men in huts 28 ft by 12 ft, two or three navvies sharing each bed, on the Hawick branch of the North British Railway, for instance. In his *The Railway Navvies* Terry Coleman quotes: 'Alexander Ramsay, an engineer, said that the huts were often verminous; he knew of one man who had found twenty-four fleas upon himself. There was no separation between the beds. In one bed slept a man and his wife and one or two children; in another a couple of young men; in a third in the same hut another man and his wife and family. In some of the huts, he said, a humane man would hardly put a pig.' ('As late as 1887, at Bere Ferris, near Devonport, some old haulks of men o'war were bought by the contractors and towed upriver for the navvies to live in.')

Antagonism was mutual, for if the navvies were unwelcomed by the local population, they felt they were outcast before they arrived, overcharged at local shops, ignored at the inn. But sometimes contact was happy, as recorded by a doctor's daughter on the outskirts of London: 'There had been much fear in the village of annoyance from the horde of Yorkshire and Lincolnshire railwaymen brought in by Fairbank, the contractor; but on the whole their conduct was very orderly, and they can hardly be sufficiently commended for their behaviour . . . A noticeable figure was "Dandy Ganger", a big north countryman, decorated with many large mother of pearl buttons and a big silver watch chain. He instantly checked all bad language in the neighbourhood of the doctor's garden. Many of the navvies brought their food or their tea cans to be heated on the kitchen range, and never once made themselves objectionable.' But five of them were killed in building as many miles of track. Fenland navvies were regarded as a cut above the others.

The doctor's daughter was a tolerant person, objectively reporting on the destruction of pretty rows of cottages, of gardens and well-beloved trees. She even thought 'The excavations were beautiful in colour' – an unusual sentiment since the commonest reference to railway building is to the scars left behind by the navvies. 'Now that the cuttings and embankments are all overgrown and covered with verdure, one can hardly realize how hideous it all looked when they were raw and glaring,' says Cecil Torr. Many of the embankments went on to produce vegetation different from that of surrounding land, usually just because the earth had been so upheaved, though sometimes aided by villagers or land-owners planting rhododendrons or other bushes to help the healing.

But the local board of directors usually had more to worry about than the appearance of the embankments. Could shareholders be counted on to pay the calls on their shares? The Callander & Oban in Scotland was

Left, pride in the local company was encouraged by decorative share certificates; this vignette comes from a share of the Middlesborough & Guisborough Railway. Right, company seals also often reflected the local scenery, such as this of the South Durham & Lancashire Union Railway.

not the only railway whose secretary discovered when requesting the first call that some who had enthusiastically signed the application forms had changed their mind. 'I beg you will be so good as to erase my name from the list of those to whom shares have been allotted,' demanded one who indignantly denied putting his name down for 50 shares. Many who paid the first call of a fifth to a third of the share price were unable or unwilling to pay later calls and forfeited their shares, so depressing the market and making it harder to raise fresh money. Rarely was a branch line built and opened with the money stated as necessary in its first Act. Acts stipulated the capital that could be raised in shares and set limits on how much could be raised by loans – companies had to go back to Parliament for fresh authority to borrow more, and to extend the period allowed for completion. Companies in difficulty had to raise so much debenture stock that from the start ordinary shareholders stood little chance of receiving dividends.

Then, contractors in those days as now came across tougher rock than bargained for and complained that bridges had to be given deeper foundations than specified. Stopping work on the line the local businessmen so badly wanted was their way of bringing pressure to bear. Conversely, if the contractor did shoddy work, payments were suspended and the much-maligned navvies went without their wages. Even where the company wished to pay the contractor on time, it often could not: 'the company are most anxious to move as slowly and cautiously as possible in all cases where money payments are required,' a Scottish contractor was told. And contractors squeezed by creditors again could not meet the weekly wage bill or even provide food rations. This happened especially after the 1866 financial crisis. Riots of navvies became commonplace; Wiveliscombe in Somerset was terrorized by a party of seventy navvies with bludgeons demanding bread and beer.

If one contractor went broke, or just gave up, another had to be found, and the cost of the two together inevitably added up to more than had been estimated. Even lines of modest length might suffer several changes of contractor. Local firms undertaking jobs beyond their experience were especially prone to collapse, and many generations-old family businesses came to an unhappy end. If the main contractor failed, there was a chain reaction among sub-contractors, some of whom might be working on other sections and thus spread the disruption. A few companies tried to build their lines by direct labour, but lack of co-ordination and experience by the team of local directors inevitably led to disaster. Only a handful succeeded, and then only on short lines and where a single key figure emerged.

A hundred and one questions, too often new to the people concerned, had to be decided. What weight rails, what quality sleepers and ballast, telegraph posts, fencing and gates? The local boards had to take technical advice from their engineer, who could be one of those holding a score of such positions up and down the country, paying only fleeting visits for which he charged a full day's fees, though others were conscientious. Some decisions needed to be taken out on the route; from Brunel downwards, engineers had assistants who took notes of the flow of water to be accommodated in a culvert, of minor changes of grade and curve, and of slippage on embankments.

Some consulting engineers were unbelievably inept; none more so than the famous Thomas Bouch, an extraordinary figure who began as staff engineer to the small St Andrew's Railway in Fife, resigned and set up in business specializing in advising country concerns needing to build and operate themselves cheaply. Despite the shocking service he normally provided he went on to greater things, including the design and construction of the first Tay Bridge that fell into the water. Thirty years before the dying Bouch heard himself condemned for the deaths of everyone travelling on the train that went down with the bridge, he had firmly established what can be seen with hindsight as a disastrous pattern of behaviour. The St Andrew's line itself had to make good many defects. The secretary of the Leven Railway, also in Fife, found it impossible to get replies from Bouch, who also missed essential meetings. The secretary wrote to the solicitor: 'I would like you to write him tomorrow, without saying it was my request, asking him positively to attend.' Everything Bouch touched went wrong: 'If it [a footbridge] is delayed much longer we will be put to half as much expense for correspondence as the bridge will cost.' And the directors of the little Crieff Junction Railway, trying to link their town with the main line 12 miles away, were made to look foolish through a string of broken promises and misunderstandings which among other things led to last-minute postponement of opening after staff had been engaged.

Then there was the correspondence with landowners, such as those who had already received payment but procrastinated over giving up possession of a field hoping to harvest a ripening crop first. All kinds of queries had to be answered: 'I have told Mr Jardine it will have to be altered or the water will take it away. The sparks from engine chimneys are caused by the blasts when they run at high speeds or when they have

'Whatjer mean – lan'slide?'

a very heavy load. In this case . . . if the buildings belonged to me I should not make any claim on the roof covering as I am sure there is no extra danger.' And 'The Coy never promised to fill in the old water course. Indeed your Clients do not now press this since . . . give him one extra share to meet him half way in the matter.' Such correspondence often has missing pieces: 'As people often make mischief perhaps it would be as well to tear this note up when you have learnt the contents.'

It was back in the board room – usually a room in an hotel or solicitor's office – that it was debated whether to build bridges and tunnels to accommodate a second track even though only a single line was to be laid initially. And it was the local directors who discussed the merits of Italianate or Gothic station designs submitted by the engineer, and determined how generous station arrangements should be. Of stations more later; decisions about them often came last, and many lines had their opening delayed while finishing touches were put to platforms and buildings. Other delays to prevent the revenue starting to flow might include the engine doing the ballasting breaking down, or signalling equipment being lost in transit, not to mention the weather.

Given the financial crises, inefficient and overworked engineers, and malpractice in circles less exalted than those of the famous Railway King, George Hudson, the total lack of experience, local jealousies and quarrels between neighbouring companies trying to defend their territories rather than open up the region, and occasionally prepared to resort even to sabotage, the wonder is that the system developed at the lightning pace it did. We could not do it today: witness the slow pace of motorway building. At least the Victorians could get action once basic agreement was reached: correspondence was answered quickly; men and equipment could usually be drafted in at a week's notice, Irishmen waiting eager to navvy; and though no company could lightly undertake going back to Parliament for further powers, there was little bureaucratic local government to contend with.

So the railways criss-crossed the country. Few places of importance in England and Wales were more than walking distance from a station by 1880, and by 1910 not even the smallest hamlet was 20 miles away. Competing routes were often wastefully built, but at least they brought trains to another valley and string of villages. Penetration of the Scottish

Highlands took longer, and then the trains connected with the ships that completed Britain's steam communications system.

Though not on the generous scale of the first grand trunk routes which went straight through all natural obstacles and sometimes had rows of streets dismantled to make way for them, country railways were still on the whole well built, commercially speaking often too well built, so that today the motorist often drives down a road far more tortuous than the parallel but now closed railway. Britain's railways as a whole cost around £40,000 a mile. Some branches economically hugging the contours were built for less than £5,000 a mile; £12-15,000 per mile would have been good value for a line of ten miles with one largish and two wayside stations but no major engineering works, and this was often more than the traffic justified. Even a single-track viaduct over a deep valley might cost over £25,000, a sum again quite out of proportion to rural traffic expectations. And this when a country stationmaster would be lucky to receive £50 a year, his cottage could be handsomely built for £200, and a company with 25 engines could employ an experienced locomotive superintendent for £200 a year.

But in quoting costs we have to remember that prices varied sharply, wages and materials both rising in the middle of the century, a mile of single broad-gauge track increasing from £1,873 in 1861 to £2,666 for roughly similar quality in 1874, to quote one example. The weight and quality of steel rails could obviously make a big difference – as it did with rolling stock. For a broad-gauge first-class coach, costing £650, re-covering the seats took 54 yards of cloth at a cost of £112, nearly as much as the cost of a six-wheeled third-class carriage with no upholstery, £145.

3 In Business

Victorian railways were run with a happy combination of free enterprise and State control through the Board of Trade, whose railway section must have been one of the most respected and best-run government departments in history. Government intervention on this scale was novel. At the very least it prevented a slapstick farce, with too many badly-built lines dangerously competing with each other. At its best it ensured that even small, rural companies had the benefit of national experience, especially in safety matters, though in later years – as we shall see – the Board's attitudes became less flexible and often caused unnecessary expenditure.

Every new railway company knew it had to conform to prescribed standards, that it could not earn a penny until it had been inspected and passed by an officer recruited from the Corps of Royal Engineers. Some of the inspecting officers became nationally known for their investigations of accidents and precautionary recommendations.

The inspector would meet the directors in friendly fashion at the local hostelry before starting work on the appointed day. He was of course provided with a special train, to direct as he pleased, and he usually required extra engines to test the strain on bridges and viaducts. He was especially concerned with signalling arrangements and with the convenience as well as safety of passengers at stations. Perhaps one time in five he refused to sanction the opening of a line until further work had been done and passed; usually he required only a few detailed amendments and left them to the care of the company. He always wrote a concise report, the document which often gives railway historians the most accurate picture of a line. Where possible he complimented the company – especially a local grassroots company – on their taste and good work, and then enjoyed the first of a series of official opening repasts. Occasionally he wrote bluntly about skimped work and cast a spell of damnation on the line and all who risked their lives – and fortunes – on it.

Opening of the Central Somerset Railway – procession in the Abbey grounds at Glastonbury.

The official opening, the day of emergence for thousands of country towns and villages between 1850 and 1880, surpassing any event before or after, might be the day after the inspection or the following week; if major work had to be done first, celebration must be postponed. Accounts of opening ceremonies, universal holidays for all, received national coverage, especially in *The Illustrated London News*, because people in business everywhere were eager to know what further places were added to the railway system; though they read as monotonously as today's accounts of bazaar openings, the spontaneity of the enthusiasm at the time is convincing.

The official train, often displaying the company's entire rolling stock, would make a symbolic trip into the country terminus with representatives from the outside world as well as local dignitaries – by invitation only. 'The populace' would be out to catch at least a distant glance of the train's arrival and to glow appreciatively at the shrill whistles of the engine. A procession would wend its way under a triumphal arch with a goodwill message to the town centre, often a fair walk away. Between two and three o'clock a trumpet would call the gentry and businessmen to their lunch, normally a joint effort between several hotels, five to eight courses followed by as many toasts. Unfailingly, the local promoters were praised for their endeavours against all obstacles: persistence had been rewarded, the prophets of doom were already confounded, but the opening was only the beginning of the bright new era. Unfailingly, bishop or vicar hoped that the Sabbath would not be disturbed by the running of excursion trains; unfailingly, a director diplomatically replied that only those Sunday trains that Post Office and public absolutely demanded would be run.

It all took at least three hours, while lesser people had sports or country dancing. The 'labouring classes', including any navvies still in the district – most would have moved on – went to their marquee for that inevitable 'cold collation' washed down with beer; tea and cakes were distributed

Swansea Station (S.W.R.) on the opening day.

Malvern Station and Hotel.

to 'females'; finally came dancing and a firework display. For country people it was all memorable and was talked about for generations to come. Exceptionally heavy rain is still occasionally referred to as 'railway weather' in Launceston, Cornwall, though no train has reached the town for years, for people were drenched when the first arrived in 1865. Commemorative medals were struck for some of the larger lines, and like mugs and ribbons are now collectors' pieces.

Starting up the regular service in the next day or two was anti-climactic, and the first revenue-earning trains were usually lightly loaded. Country people took time to work the train services into their own routines, to realize the life-changing potential. But almost always the railway made real impact by the end of its first month. The hastening of the mails and the drop in the price of coal and other key commodities brought in from other districts were first noticed, and steadily more people came and went, expanded their horizons: the horse-drawn traffic in the streets of market towns noticeably increased and hotels found new importance.

Hotel visitors included meat-buyers from city wholesale butchers; their purchases of course put up local prices, sometimes causing hardship, as in Cornwall with the opening of a through line 'to England' in 1859, when a sizeable proportion of the pilchard catch – the miners' cheap protein – was also diverted. Some East Anglian hay had always gone to London to feed horses and the cows then kept in and near the city, but now merchants bought it by the trainload – even though the railway meant London could look to the country for its daily fresh milk. Within a few weeks of opening, milk churns would be despatched from most country stations; the value of milk to the farmer depended on how far he was from a station. In 1881 it was reckoned that Derbyshire farmers could obtain 1s a gallon for liquid milk sent to a city (they had to pay rail carriage out of this) compared with 8d a gallon if it had to be turned into butter or cheese, a labour-consuming business with a long wait for cash.[1] So the careful handling of milk churns, preventing them standing for hours in the sun, along with a growing range of fruit and vegetables (in both directions, since local produce was partly balanced by increased imports of oranges, bananas and other fruits), became daily routine.

But perhaps nowhere did the arrival of trains more thoroughly affect habits than in the village pub where local brews suddenly looked expensive beside Burton and other mass-produced lines. Never had the village economy received such a jolt. Some local breweries closed down – as did many village shops as more people travelled to town; and mail-order shopping took roots. The railway was a boon, its power immediately

1. Around 1850 when the general price of milk was 8d to 10d a gallon, producers in Liverpool had earned 1s to 1s 4d because of local scarcity; they quickly complained about the drop in the rate when merchants organized wholesale rail imports. The coming of the railways had many curious effects. So much milk was exported from the South West that it became scarce locally, a woman complaining at a protest meeting in the Devon village of Broad Clyst that she could not 'buy a ha'porth worth'. So far as livestock were concerned, the benefit of railways was measured in weight saving; the old drover method of getting Norfolk beef to London was cheaper than the train charges, but on the road a bullock lost 28 lb and a sheep 7 lb. Rail saved around £1 net a beast, and the quickness of trains made it easier to match supply to demand. Long-distance droving seldom survived more than a few weeks after the opening of a railway, the traditional Scottish trails being cut short at railheads such as Lairg as soon as the steam age arrived. The growing reliance of agriculture on railways has to be seen against the background of the passing of the Corn Laws, disruption caused by the Crimean war, cattle plague in 1865–6 and the general depression in agriculture thereafter, including a series of disastrous seasons in the 1870s. Though corn and beef continued to receive

obvious, bringing a small place self-confidence. But usually a single railway had a monopoly and did not have to be generous; rural stations saw only three to six trains daily in each direction, most of them stopping at all stations. As on main lines, third-class and 'Parliamentary' passengers (Parliament had laid down that there must be a daily service at only a penny a mile over every line) were frequently confined to the least convenient trains, those starting early and maybe shunting en route. Third-class travel might also cost a penny or else show a prestigious differential at a penny farthing. The second-class mile was 1½d or so, the first-class 2d to 3d. In the early years a considerable proportion of first-class passengers loaded the family carriage onto the train on country journeys.

Throughout the land pressure was exerted for a better service, the ironing out of those irritating anomalies that have always collected round the running of railways. The first to complain about the service and connections were often the local board of directors. After all the trouble of building their line they may have decided it would be too much responsibility to operate it themselves, and leased it to the nearest main-line company for a proportion of the gross takings. Local companies with a good line to lease might get 45 or even 50 per cent of the receipts, but in rural backwaters the deal was more often 60 or even 65 per cent to the operating big-body. Few directors who had sunk savings into the local railway could feel it was being properly fostered by a large concern with many irons in the fire – especially if the sums received were not adequate to pay the

much of the public comment, Britain became steadily more a dairying country, and in this the railways certainly played a vital role, carrying the new feeds including cotton-seed cake and maize cheaply imported. Milk-carryings on the Midland increased six times between 1872 and 1880, and on most lines doubled again in 10 or 15 years straddling the turn of the century. Horticulture was also revolutionized, beginning directly by the railways compulsorily purchasing the land occupied by growers in and around London and a few other big centres. Many growers who went on to become famous used their handsome compensation to start on a larger scale near a well-served station. Others financed improvements out of money paid in damages for viaducts that shaded the ground or for black smoke emitted by locomotives. For the latter a grower in Stratford, Essex, obtained £500 and another £800 eight years later from the Great Eastern Railway which – perhaps because its books did not balance that happily – did more than many lines to encourage horticulture with fair rates and reliable service; the rapid growth of the fruit and vegetable market at Stratford itself was one result.

Hardly a country station was without its milk churns in the days when fresh milk sent to the nearest large town might fetch as much again as that turned laboriously into butter or cheese. In the top picture farm workers and railway staff pose at Highbridge in Somerset. Every new line brought joy for the local farmers if not the railway's shareholders; the lower picture is of Calvert on the Great Central's London extension, the last main line in Britain, shortly after opening in 1899.

interest on capital, rates and such like. One village railway, the Killin on Loch Tay, suddenly received no payment at all because the Caledonian alleged receipts were below the minimum allowed for in the agreement: and this a few months after opening in 1886.

Loading the special at the end of a Welsh fair at day's end; the scene could equally well have been at dozens of English, Scottish and Irish country stations.

So even if they had not intended to become practical railwaymen, some boards felt obliged to take over. Others saw from the start that to earn enough money they must equip and staff the show themselves. Engines could be hired from the big neighbour, but at 10d a mile for passengers and 1s for goods that again left little prospect of profit. The secretary of the 18¾-mile Peebles Railway explained to his directors why they should take the plunge:

Gentlemen acquainted only with the working of great companies cannot form a proper estimate of economical working by a smaller company. They are accus-

39

Valuable business at Staverton on what is now the preserved Dart Valley Railway in Devon, as recorded by a local enthusiast.

tomed to see everything on a great scale and without an attempt at economy. Their undertakings are too large for the supervision of one man and the oversight is broaken [sic] down into a variety of departments without any unity of the control. It is found that two or three mechanics with a bench at the side of the engine shed and a foot lathe are amply sufficient for all the ordinary repairs of locomotives and carriages.

So the farmers, solicitors and other country gentlemen had to choose their own engine; and to make the right choice for the route and the traffic was crucial. Taking the internal combustion engine for granted, we forget how varied could be the performance from steam machines of theoretically similar design and power, and how totally dependent a whole valley might be on the engine driver's ability to coax a temperamental lady up a steep bank. Railway histories are littered with instances of traffic – and revenue – being ground to a halt, or small companies reaching despair over the cost of coal or repairs, through the use of unsuitable engines. But how were a group of country gentry expected to make a judgement, especially if the experts were at variance?

The temptation to buy cheap or secondhand was often irresistible: a good new tender locomotive usually cost £2,000. Money for even a secondhand bargain might not be there, but one of the shareholders would make a personal loan – or the machine might be bought on hire purchase from its previous owner. Even larger concerns did not always own the engines they used; those with chronically disordered finances like the Somerset & Dorset had their machines seized for security and had to run them displaying their new owners' plates.

Expert maintenance meant much, and depended on the man in charge, the locomotive superintendent if the company had half a dozen or more machines. He was usually only second in importance to the man who ran the whole line, the general manager or, more usual with smaller concerns, the secretary or clerk to the board. Some companies, especially in Scotland, retained the services of an outstanding manager-secretary for a generation, paying him liberally and allowing him to undertake consultancy work for others. Others, like the Midland & South Western Junction, rose in performance and morale during the periods that railwaymen destined for greater authority – Sam Fay in this case – stopped with them. The poorer the line, the harder to get the right man, and not surprisingly the narrow-gauge railways of Ireland built with the help of Government grant to relieve distressed areas had to endure inexperience.

Sometimes the day-to-day management was taken over by a receiver, such as James Haldane of Edinburgh who became judicial factor managing the Girvan & Portpatrick Railway in south-west Scotland in place of the directors (in 1879). Receivers were managers to keep things going, not liquidators. The only way Haldane could see for the struggling line to survive was for it to take over its own operation. But some shareholders thought this too risky and Haldane had to fight his right to take the action in court. A Mr Read, managing as receiver the Eastern & Midlands Railway, part of what was later to become the cross-country Midland & Great Northern Joint, found himself accused of a variety of sins, including hiring rolling stock without having means to pay for it. The debenture holders took him to court, but he too won and kept the line running. Nor were these isolated cases. Companies were always in court, in and out of chancery, producing schemes of rearrangement to keep credit at bay, fighting each other over territorial arrangements and commissions. Many companies large and small spent as much in legal fees as they received from the Post Office for the carriage of mails, and that contract was always seen as a cornerstone of traffic and gave the Post Office the right to determine schedules.

In the end it had to be the daily takings rather than the expenses that determined whether a company would succeed or not. The line with strong and growing traffic could eventually hope to put its affairs in order. The best branch-line businesses were those with regular mineral or manu-factured-goods traffic on top of the ordinary carriage of miscellaneous items: a good line might take three times as much revenue from goods as from passengers. When the wool trade was still prosperous in the Dart Valley, Buckfastleigh's freight revenue exceeded that of any main-line goods station on the South Devon Railway. Nationally, freight overtook passenger takings in 1852, and all good railwaymen preached that goods provided the bread and butter, passengers only the jam.[1] Much of the goods traffic was new: to quote the Royal Commission on Railways, 'In considering the improvement of goods traffic, it is very difficult to in-stitute any comparison with the past, because the introduction of the rail-way system has entirely altered all the conditions of that traffic, and has enabled industry and trade to spring up which, without railways, could have had no existence.'

And whatever the traffic, however sadly the hopes in the prospectus had been dashed, the costs went on remorselessly. Even a new signal lamp at £2 18s 6d in 1865 exceeded a country stationmaster's weekly salary, and any goods wagon cost an average £7 a year in maintenance. In the same year evidence was given to a Royal Commission on Railways show-ing the average cost of running trains on the Great Western's varied sys-tem (per train mile, in pence)

Maintenance of way	6.35
Locomotive	6.75
Carriage and waggons	3.37
Carrying account (management)	6.91
General charges	2.74
Compensation	0.45

1. Unique among Europe's railway systems, Britain's freight business has declined until now passengers bring in over half the revenue. Therein lies the problem of mounting losses and curtailed services.

Disbursements	0.13
Fire insurance premiums	0.07
General office expenses	
(directors and general manager)	0.62
Government duty on passenger receipts	1.12
Taxes	1.10

With miscellaneous items that totalled 2s 7.1d (13p) a mile. Top drivers then received 7s 6d a day, plus 6d a day or £10 a year premium for good behaviour, the lowest-grade driver 4s 6d a day and goods drivers 5s – but the fuel bill was nearly twice as high for goods as passenger trains.

Many local lines found themselves unable to cover such costs with enough over for depreciation and emergencies plus the very substantial sums needed to service capital. These lines had often been built, with the reckless optimism of ignorance, to far too expensive a standard, sometimes in the hope that the route could be extended to form a through one, with greater potential, at some future date. Promoters usually over-estimated country traffic potentials, as they seem to have under-estimated many urban ones. People were slow to realize how urban Britain was becoming. It was the initial decision to build lines serving sparsely-populated areas virtually to main-line standards, instead of on a rudimentary 'light railway' basis that was wrong, though as we shall see in chapter 8 even some light railway companies too had to sell out to main-line concerns at half the cost of construction. Not, it should be remembered, that main-line companies made the profit, paid the dividends, of the more successful canals: few railways paid more than 6 per cent, though no higher return on capital could be obtained than that from the most profitable railways. Dividends declined steadily in the last third of the century. Nationally, working expenses as a proportion of total receipts rose from the 50 per cent achieved on all good lines to over 60 per cent. This was partly due to rising wages, partly to Government control on fares and freight rates, factors not anticipated when companies were building up their capital debt. The whole system, like much of British industry then, was over-capitalized, perhaps the price we had to pay for being first in the field.

So the man in charge of the ailing country railway would anxiously

"Ow about a search party or summat, Zeb? She were due in at a quarter after five last evenin'"

watch daily traffic receipts. Well over half the passenger income came from third-class journeys and only 5–10 per cent from first. An order for a special train at 5s a mile, or a cattle special after a great market day perhaps earning a little more, would bring some relief, but still two-thirds to three-quarters of the total revenue might be taken by routine working expenses – too much. The manager held off creditors under the monthly reconciliation with the Railway Clearing House which apportioned the charges on through journeys between the lines concerned. But sooner or later it became clear to officials and directors of too many lines that the task was hopeless. The railway might have brought prosperity to their valley, but not to them.

To return to Cecil Torr's comments on the Moretonhampstead branch in Devon: 'Financially the railway was a failure. There was a capital of £105,000 in shares and £35,000 in debentures, but the expenditure was £155,000. And the company was amalgamated with the South Devon Railway on 1 July 1872, the £105,000 in shares being exchanged for £52,500 in ordinary stock, and the £35,000 in debentures for £35,000 in debenture stock. And then the South Devon company was amalgamated with the Great Western company on 1 February 1876, each £100 of South Devon ordinary stock and each £100 of South Devon debenture stock for £100 of Great Western 5 per cent debenture stock. Thus £100 in shares came down to £32 10s in stock.' And the local pride went too, especially as almost all such takeovers were followed by big improvement schemes to emphasize how run-down the thing had become.

While Victoria was still on the throne most locally-created lines sold out for between 40 and 60 per cent of their cost, and few were left to be amalgamated when all regular railways were compulsorily grouped into the Big Four in 1923. One such survival, curiously after its earlier troubles, was Killin's little village line, its sole purpose being to connect the lochside settlement with the Oban branch. It refused point-blank the first offer of £1 of LMSR stock for each £100 of its own; the secretary did not at first understand how the newly-formed LMSR came into the picture anyway, though he went on to negotiate and eventually obtained £8 per £100. When sending a copy of the accounts in handwriting he apologized: 'I am without a typist' but the Killin line never afforded anything as expensive as a typewriter.

It was not of course only the independent lines that made a loss. The country branch lines started by main-line companies also lost heavily. Even many main-line wayside stations hardly covered the wages of their staff. The North British Railway's Border Union line had eleven stations in the lean, windswept miles between Hawick and Carlisle. In 1920, the peak year for railway traffic, before the age of mass motoring and with few buses hardy enough to search there for traffic, their takings were:

	PASSENGER £	GOODS £
Stobs	1,016	247
Shankend	147	419
Riccarton Jct	529	1,177
Steele Road	381	181
Newcastleton	2,250	1,425
Kershope Foot	281	131
Penton	1,029	1,425
Riddings Jct	1,262	1,025
Scotch Dyke	486	271
Longtown	4,550	9,025
Harker	249	646

Cecil Torr's Lustleigh. Note the gardens.

The Killin train after the LMSR had taken over, depriving the village of the management of its railway.

Two of these, be it noted, were junctions, so that only part of their revenue would be for the branch lines.

But let us end with the story of a country yet main-line railway whose shareholders eventually received £347 for each £100 invested: the Salisbury & Yeovil, locally-inspired and controlled, though operated as part of the London & South Western's trunk route to Exeter. Among its shareholders was a journalist, Louis H. Ruegg, who explained: 'The foundation of success is to be found in the geography of the line. It is the straightest way to the point arrived at, and admits of no competition. The directors were not exposed in any great degree to the fatal temptation of the class, to throw out branches; which, sometimes real "feeders" have, generally proceed to be sources of embarrassment; first financially, requiring the raising of capital at a disadvantage; next in the traffic, by producing delays to the main trains. Once only did they listen for a moment to a suggestion to "throw out a spur". They proposed to give notice for powers to make a line from Gillingham to Bruton, a length

Over a generation later, in 1965, the Killin train still comprises a single coach, though now hauled by a new British Railways Standard 2-6-4T.

of some 16 miles; but they fortunately withdrew, and what they escaped may, in part, be estimated by those who know anything of the history of that most unfortunate of railways, the Somerset & Dorset ... One town upon the line which might fairly claim a closer connection with it – Shaftesbury – requires, and some day will have, no doubt, about three miles of rail to connect it with the main line; but the directors held their hands even in this case, and their firmness in resisting the making of any branch at all was unquestionably one of the causes of success.'

Mercifully for those who might have been persuaded to invest in it, Ruegg's prediction was wrong and Shaftesbury never had a railway. The town still suffers.

4 The Village Station

The station was the place where the railway greeted its local customers and took their money, the doorway through which important people right up to royalty would pass on visits to the district, the storeplace for every kind of commodity precious and bulky in transit from town to country and vice versa. It was also the place where news came in from the outside world, either by telegraph – provided on the railways long before post offices began transmitting telegrams (Greenwich time was also checked daily) – or by newspaper or word of mouth. It was the place where every piece of invention of the Victorian age could first be seen – from the railway's own telegraph instrument and signalling system, newest engine or crane, to threshing machines, mangles, toilet cisterns and bicycles. And here troops would have arrived to quell disturbances or uprising, while local organizers of the Anti-Corn-Law-League and early unions went off to national gatherings. Here, too, came Gladstone and other politicians to whip up support.

Just how important the station was in the life of the community can be gauged from the numerous stretches of approach road and lane that were improved at the ratepayers' expense – widened, often given pavements which look particularly incongruous leading to nowhere today, and lit with gas lamps. In many cases, the gas came from new works with their own coal siding beside the station.

The local population took intense interest in the siting and design of their station: 'I can quite understand the anxiety of Mr Hine and his friends to have the station close to his mill, but I do feel very much annoyed that they have made it a party matter.' And when it was being built each evening knots of the curious would gather to see how the contractors were doing. Many companies were more concerned to save expensive earthworks and gradients that would be hard on locomotives

The country station in the valley with two push-and-pull auto-car trains
crossing ... the scene many of us perhaps remember best. The place is
Thorverton on the Exe Valley line, the time early morning on 12 March 1960.
First train in always last out at crossing stations on single-line branches. Hence
the down-train, with few passengers, arrived first to allow a sharp getaway by
the Exeter-bound one carrying workers and schoolchildren to Exeter. Both
have locomotives of the GW's 0-4-2 1400 class. This was once a busy branch
line, its most active years perhaps unusually being after nationalization when

services were increased with occasional semi-fasts missing some of the halts, full Sunday through trains to the coast, and a Saturdays-only late service from Exeter to Tiverton on which latecomers often had to stand. Thorverton had no bus service and provided many passengers. In addition to its little goods yard, it had a private siding to a mill, and the route from the junction at Stoke Canon to the mill survived a few years after the rest of the line closed.

than to carry the inhabitants of country towns and villages to their own doorsteps. So hill-top towns like Torrington and South Molton (chapter 7) in Devon had their stations in the valley a mile or more away, and even where the lie of the land was easy the railway usually petered out before village housing began. It was one thing to pay for the demolition of property at the approaches to London; another to go to the expense of saving country people a short walk. The builders of main lines thought they could tap traffic from even the largest villages without bending the route; if the wayside station was more than five or six miles away the word 'Road' might be added to its name. And often two villages were served by a joint station named after both but convenient for neither. Some companies consulted local opinion about situation and design; others went their own way and the public got what it did.

Sometimes the public received more station than its custom justified, especially where served by a proud little independent company with great belief in its own importance. Newmarket in Suffolk had a station of incredible opulence, at the end of the 20 miles of the Newmarket & Chesterford Railway. The Italianate station house, only one of three major buildings, has been described by one writer as a 'Baroque orangery' and another as 'a succession of tall finely hooded windows, interspersed with coupled Ionic columns, all rising above a deep cornice to richly orna-

*Narrow-gauge prodigality. Aughnacloy on the Clogher Valley Railway in
Ireland (above) and (left) one of the Lynton & Barnstaple's villa-type stations
at Chelfham, still too ambitious for the very limited local traffic.*

mented caps . . . seven bays in all, in ashlar stone.' Richmond in Yorkshire
had a kind of monastic Gothic terminus, 'astonishingly medieval with
its arcaded and buttressed entrance, mullioned windows and tall angled
chimneys in dark freestone.' It is perhaps the best known of country
stations to have a preservation order clapped on it, although now used
as a builders' merchants it is little seen.[1]

Some stations quickly seen to be over-ambitious were the result of
genuine mistakes in forecasting traffic volume: Crieff in Perthshire for
instance. Others were built as headquarters for local companies later taken

---

1. Gordon Biddle's description of Richmond in his *Victorian Stations* continues: 'A remarkable
two bay trainshed in glass and iron covered the platforms and three tracks do duty as station and
carriage shed combined, and its gabled ends were decorated with herring-bone timbering, shell
panel openings and exquisite barge boards.' Designed by George T. Andrews and built in 1846,
it blended perfectly with the superb landscape beside the River Swale as it winds round Richmond.
After closure in 1969 – it had been a busy branch till the end – the Historic Buildings Council
contributed £7,000 Government money, and local people most of the remainder of the £50,000
needed, for restoration. There were hopes it might become a carriage museum; it certainly deserved a
better fate than use as merchant's depot.

53

Highland extravaganza. Though the Kyle of Lochalsh line passed close by, the tiny spa of Strathpeffer demanded its own railway; a station with a roof worthy of a town five times as large protected the occasional passengers alighting from mixed trains. The locomotive is a former Highland Railway 4-4-0T.

Timber cladding on the grand scale at Kidderminster.

over: the Cambrian Railways inherited from its constituents four remark-
ably oversized ranges of buildings, at Ellsesmere, Oswestry, Llanidloes
(a solidity especially out of place) and Welshpool.

At the other extreme, station buildings could be mere cottages for the
stationmaster, with one room, divided into staff and public sections, for
railway business. *Cottages ornés*, often derived from J. C. Loudon's *Ency-
clopaedia of Cottage, Farm and Villa Architecture*, published in 1833,
linked the new form of transport with the homely and familiar. Local
stone was usually used though there might be timber cladding, as on a
grand scale at Kidderminster, still open. Hundreds of stations were of
individual designs deep in local tradition. But as time went on the principal engineers and companies created their own styles. Brunel was as
interested in the details of station design as in laying out a major line
or creating a steamship; like most of his work, his stations were outside
ordinary traditions. He probably introduced the use of standard drawings
and possibly even standard units for his wooden stations in the west of
England; in their later years those with all-over roofs became much
photographed by enthusiasts.

Other railway architects included those better known in other fields,
like Sir William Tite, or oddballs such as Francis Thompson who built

*Handsomely decorated, perhaps to impress Queen Victoria, Aboyne on the
Great North of Scotland Railway's branch to Ballater for Balmoral.*

a series of highly individual stone stations for the North Midland Railway, ranging from Eckington's Italianate villa with a handsome rotunda of an entrance with a conical sugar-bowl top, to a riotous Jacobean Ambergate. Thompson does not figure as an architect outside the railway world and is believed to have been a London tailor with a design flair put to good use during the railway boom.

The variety of the early stations was endless, even apparently similar stations on the same line being built with local stones of different colours. As Christian Barman pointed out in the *British Transport Review* as far back as 1950, it was not in the famous city termini but at the country stations that 'the special idiom of railway architecture is found in its strongest and purest form. No country in the world has a collection of minor stations that can begin to compare with ours for sheer quality.' The purity of the original designs survived because of light wear and tear – no need to replace equipment or enlarge offices.

But regular travellers came to associate certain parts of the country with a particular type of station. The London & South Western developed a distinct style of plain houses with gables overlooking the platform; it went on building these in the forty years taken to extend the route from Basingstoke to Padstow and a number survive. The South Eastern Railway, ever parsimonious, went on building wooden hut stations of 1842 vintage till the last years of the century. Wood, though it could be pleasing, was more often seen as an economy substitute in the financially tougher times after the 1850s. And inevitably local stone was ousted, in stations as in other buildings, by the mass-produced building materials the railways carted throughout the country: the Great Northern, serving the Peterborough brickfields, led the way in killing vernacular architecture and was duly accused by *The Illustrated London News* of avoiding the use of 'the more costly kinds of materials and workmanship'.

Buildings at terminal stations were usually placed across the buffer stops; at through stations the main range was halfway down one platform, often with only a primitive shelter on the other platform. The roof at many termini was there more to shelter the coaches stored overnight than for the benefit of passengers.

Though passengers might have to buy their tickets while standing in a draughty corridor, the accommodation even at village stations could

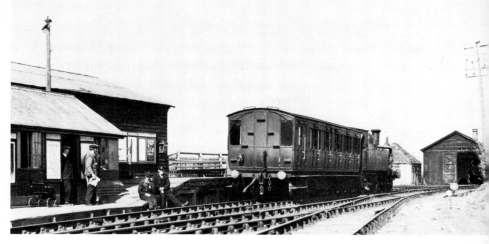

If you had to guess which railway this rural outfit belonged to, you would start in the far corners of the kingdom. In fact it was a country outpost – Brill – of the Metropolitan.

include first and second (later third) class general waiting-rooms with separate ladies' room with toilets – the famous sign at Callander has been preserved: '2nd Class Ladies' – (Gentlemen were usually accommodated in an outbuilding or odd corner at the end of the range), stationmaster's office and telegraph room, and parcels office in which tickets, date-punch and booking records might be housed. Extra rooms for engineering or signalling staff looking after sections of route might be needed, and as we have seen at Helston, even a remote country terminus could have its refreshment room. Outside, W. H. Smith might have their bookstalls even at places of very modest population.

Telegraphs and bookstalls both brought extra importance to stations. By 1868 some 1,226 stations, many of them deep in the country, had public telegraph facilities, and another 738 had the telegraph for railway use only. Instruments cost between £20,000 and £50,000 and were the wonder of the age. Telegraph lines were generally the property of a handful of telegraph companies who paid rental to the railways. The companies had their own well-paid staffs at large places, but at country stations the railway undertook the working, including delivery of messages, usually free within a mile of the station and 1s a mile on horseback beyond, though messages costing over 5s would not be delivered without express instructions. The telegraphic message itself usually cost 1s. The railways undertook where possible to use specific porters on deliveries.

The development of the service became a national debating point in the 1860s and it was nationalized as a Post Office monopoly in 1870, public opinion being that the Post Office had not abused its monopoly with mails. Also, many railway stations were thought too far outside their towns and villages. The Post Office undertook to establish a telegraph in every office where money-order business was transacted, and as part of the agreement with the railways was to allow railway messages to be carried free – hardly bargaining for the 1,600,000 reached by 1891. (Railway companies did not fail to point out to their stationmasters that staffs should not expect to send free personal messages such as those saying they would be late home from work.) Later the railway developed its own independent telephone system, the wires generally attached to poles freed from Post Office telegraphs, which were steadily re-routed beside roads for readiness of access for repairs, and of course to avoid paying rental to the railways.

Almost toylike among the trees, and at peak times almost as busy as a model railway station when its owner is in session, Ventnor on the Isle of Wight.

The railway station where the papers arrived was the natural place to sell them, and W. H. Smith's business expanded so rapidly (185 stations served as early as 1862) that it covered nearly all England. In the 1870s and 1880s a high proportion of national papers and magazines were collected by customers or delivery boys from station bookstalls, many of which also sported small circulating libraries whose stock was regularly exchanged by train with books from headquarters in London. One of the familiar stories of the newspaper and book trade is how Smith's lost a major part of their railway contracts but opened a branch in every town

Rustic charm at Bourton-on-the-Water (GWR)
and at Sandon (North Staffordshire Railway).

concerned in time to preserve continuity, of course reducing the early-morning pilgrimages to stations. The success of Smith's in building town-centre businesses spurred others to follow and thus the station ceased to be the place for changing your library book and despatching a wire.

But the passenger station was a small part of the total. A key building was the signalbox: though the electronic links with neighbouring stations were occasionally housed in the passenger station with points and signals controlled from a ground-frame open to the elements, it was usually thought prudent to give the signalmen privacy and a view of operations as well as to bring everything under cover at one place. Signalboxes might be on the platform or a short distance down the line. A separate hut was

Unstaffed halt. The notice was displayed in every GWR auto-train. What it in fact said was that passengers joining at halts bought their tickets en route. When photographed in 1961, the busy halt at Halberton in Devon displayed train departure times; but this was rare. At Borrobol on the route to the far north the Highland Railway provided real economy with just gravel at ground level for platform. An old coach for shelter on the Thaxted branch.

usually provided for lamps and oil storage: a station of any size had its lamp boy.

At a terminal or junction station, there was probably a locomotive shed, perhaps only just large enough to squeeze in the single engine stabled overnight, but designed and built with loving care, like that for the Sudbury train at Marks Tey, at right angles to the East Anglian main line and now converted into a home. Four or five tenders would normally be invited from builders; intent on good quality, the directors of the Tees Valley Railway rejected the cheapest tender for their shed at Middleton-in-Teesdale, and bargained with another builder. This like many another country locomotive shed came to have an incredible range of machines, many of them elderly, pass through its doors, and its two sets of enginemen must have become minor experts on steam power. Larger centres would have two or more tracks and space and tools for minor repairs as well as routine servicing. Since few such sheds have survived, it has taken the grand replica of a Victorian brick locomotive depot built by David Shepherd, the wildlife and railway artist, for his East Somerset Railway, to remind us how fine the proportions and materials could be.

It was at these engine sheds that the daily routine of branch lines began, fires being raised before passengers for the first train were awake. It might be twenty hours before the final ashes were dropped into the pit, even on branches that seemed to close for a long night; and if a repair was urgent, one or two men would hammer away through the small hours. Facilities outside were bound to include coal storage (at country depots the coal usually had to be unloaded by hand) and a water pipe, normally supplied from the railway's own water-tank placed high up on a building or on its own tower. Selecting and maintaining the water supply, so vital to steam engines, was one of the stationmaster's key responsibilities. Riparian disputes were common, as were mechanical troubles where pumping was needed – diesel engines were introduced for this purpose decades before they powered trains. Sometimes the railway supplied water to surrounding areas.

Watching what passed through the goods shed would tell you the state of the district's economy. Four to ten wagons might stand on a single track inside the shed, which had doors at both ends. The platform was a transhipment area between rail truck and horse-drawn cart and later lorry, but it might be weeks before bulk arrivals were distributed and it would seldom be empty. Checking the goods in and out, quoting terms and writing way-bills employed several men and boys at stations serving sizeable populations even when ten or twelve hour days were the norm; they had an office, perhaps built as a lean-to against the main building.

In the goods shed a small crane supplemented muscle and barrow. Large loads such as pieces of machinery would be lifted by the larger crane outside or rolled off a truck on to a ramp next to the buffers. Consignors had to know what cranes were available at which stations and would ask their local staff to consult the *Railway Clearing House Handbook of Railway Stations* for the weights that could be handled: 'Most Companies have travelling cranes with a lifting power of five tons and upwards, which can be removed from one station to another, as circumstances require.' But that did not stop oversize loads arriving; every railwayman had his stock of tales of that kind. The *Handbook* also detailed which stations dealt with 'Furniture Vans, Carriages, Portable Engines, and Machines on Wheels' and which kept on hand a supply of horse boxes and vans for prize cattle, the British of course always affording greater comfort to these than the run of livestock. In riding and hunting country there would always be a horse box, a four-wheeled vehicle with a compartment for rider and family on hand, and the daily takings would be handsomely swollen if a customer turned up, perhaps only ten minutes before a passenger train was due to leave. But livestock in any quantity would be loaded and unloaded at the cattle pens provided with their own track, and at stations every dozen or so miles in good agricultural country further cattle and sheep pens showed where the local market or fair was held. Many monthly fairs and markets changed locations after the opening of the railway.

Coal normally had its own siding or two, with areas of yard rigidly allocated to the various merchants who would also have their offices or primitive huts. A village of 2,500 people would support up to six different merchants, and in many places two or three survived the 1939–45 war; a co-operative society might unload coal by mechanical apparatus used on a circuit of ten country stations, spending a couple of days at each a month.

There might be between four and ten tracks for public goods and coal, and except at the smallest stations a headshunt to allow shunting to take place independently of the main running line. Additional sidings might serve the warehouse of grain or fodder merchants, a few of which (where the rails remain open for other traffic) still receive occasional wagons, for a gasworks, a council engineering depot, a milk depot, mill or brewery. Probably a quarter to a third of country stations, probably over half of the terminal ones, served some industry that may have preceded the railway's arrival or soon followed it. Not that the railway always spelt expansion, for some mills and breweries proved unable to withstand the competition from elsewhere. By the end of Victoria's reign there were thousands of mouldering factories and warehouses beside country stations – killed by the railway itself.

Many builders and contractors had their yards beside a station, though few were large enough to justify their own siding and had to transport bricks, drainpipes and tiles from the public yard. Quarries and small mines once abounded and were usually rail-served, with sidings often adjoining or close to stations; like brewing, stone quarrying has been especially subject to concentration into big units.

Some companies had their locomotive and other works in the country, those at St Blazey in Cornwall, Highbridge on the Somerset & Dorset, and Inverurie on the Great North of Scotland, for example, each employing several hundred skilled men drawn from villages and hamlets around.

As well as the stationmaster's house, there might be several cottages for railwaymen, or even complete terraces with shops at remote locations where engines and trains were stabled. Reedsmouth, near Hexham, and Waskerley, on Muggleswick Moor, Tyneside, are two North-Eastern examples of complete railway villages with a highly distinctive community life. The latter had its own church and school, the railway paying the schoolmaster as it did in several remote Scottish places. At Gorton on the West Highland Railway, the school was on the platform, its pupils being brought by train from lineside cottages at various points on the Moor of Rannoch unconnected by road; the children's mothers were given free travel to do their shopping in Fort William. At Rannoch station itself even the church was on the platform, a signalman being beadle. But at Riccarton on the Waverley route the railway settlement lacked a place of worship so the railway provided a church train, on alternate Sundays, to Hawick and Newcastleton. At Kyle of Lochalsh the council met on the platform and the refreshment room acted as 'local' long after the last night's train had departed.

Station pubs are part of local lore in all parts of rural Britain. Those on the Highland Railway north of Inverness often did roaring trade when trains were snowbound at stations, especially in later years when under union rules men stranded away from home found themselves on continuous overtime and had no need to economize. In tourist areas the station was the obvious place for a major new hotel; the railway ran its own in a few country places but generally encouraged private enterprise with cheap rent and other attractions. Such hotels often had their own covered way to the platforms. Keswick is one of a number of resorts whose top hotel now looms forlornly outside a deserted station, the covered way a dead-end greenhouse. Large-scale tea-rooms were a natural adjunct for Scottish termini at beauty spots such as Ballater. Several remote Scottish and North-East England stations attracted a post office to their very platform. Post boxes were of course universal, serviced by postmen meeting mail trains, and telephone kiosks became common at larger stations; the familiar blue 'You may telephone from here' notice offered the railway's Post Office line at smaller places.

Furnishings and fittings were often as individual as the companies; the Furness Railway seats with their delightful cast-iron squirrels, the LSWR twisted lamp columns and the finials of the Great Western's signals; nameboards, 'Gentlemen', loading gauges, weighbridges, all varied. General waiting-rooms were often bleak with long hard benches an inconvenient distance from an immovably solid table but with a welcoming fire. Fires might blaze in the ladies' room, the waiting-room on the other platform, the stationmaster's office, parcels room, goods office and signal-box, even at a very minor traffic centre. Even the fire-irons are collector's pieces today.

The waiting-room would certainly be decorated with pictures of beauty spots on the company's own system, though by mutual exchange the billboards outside would include posters of other railways, Irish as well as British. Railway sites were vital to advertisers, even the risers of the steps up to footbridges endlessly declaring 'Virol'. As well as posters, the timetable would be displayed – it was British Railways who ceased printing those vast broadsheets on which the stationmaster underlined

Furness Railway squirrel seat and LNWR two-sided platform clock at Denbigh, North Wales.

his own station's line in red crayon – and a rack of excursion leaflets, grabbed by children as well as potential ticket buyers. Except at stations with a bookstall you could only expect to buy the company's own time-tables, guides and monthly magazine, a penny for the ordinary and tup-pence for the insurance edition. Automatic machines were universal but were standardized at an early stage. Nor must one forget the gardens. Most lines ran best-kept-garden competitions and the hanging baskets, tubs, formal flower beds or larger areas, maybe including even a garden pool between platforms at some country junction stations, could receive devoted care in an age when headquarters would cheerfully accept a sta-tionmaster's order for a truckful of soil.

Most stations covered several acres, a little world on its own, with its particular sounds and smells, routines and traditions. At the turn of the century a station might be the first place in the area to be electrically lit, by its own private supply system, but generally the whole thing was so solidly permanent, so self-contained, that change to the lighting, even to a signal or a seat, was hardly thought of until closure or until the clock and other fittings had to be taken down because their value had increased too much as collector's pieces. In this continuity lay both charm and dis-comfort for later users.

But it is the range and variety of country stations rather than their longevity that is astonishing. And the number. Probably around 5,000 of Great Britain's 7,000-odd passenger stations served essentially rural communities, though this figure includes halts as well as stations proper. Halts, or haltes as they were first termed, were pioneered in the early 1900s by the Great Western, and that system alone had several hundred in 1939, with examples on all but 27 of its 150-odd branches. Stopping points to attract traffic between orthodox stations, they were merely marked by ballast and sign posts, but platforms the length of a single coach were built later. Most were unstaffed and you bought your ticket on the train – or possibly from a pub or shop. Other railways serving rural areas followed the GW's example, and in the motor age trains stopped close to many communities they had ignored when steam had a monopoly. Some halts attracted more custom than the neighbouring stations, but they could be opened and closed with little cost; the several thousand pounds considered necessary to build even the cheapest station properly discouraged experiment.

Few surviving country lines now have staff, except perhaps at peak periods at their terminus. The garden has disappeared and the signals too, since goods traffic is usually concentrated at a few main-line stations and there are never two passenger trains on the line together. The buildings rot until demolished and replaced by simple bus-type shelters, perhaps the ultimate indignity but practical. Ironically one station, Stonehouse in Gloucestershire, has lost its passenger trains because the buildings were made the subject of a preservation order and British Rail will not afford to maintain them, though ready to demolish them and provide a shelter.

Many station yards now lie weedy and deserted. Others come to life when the coal merchant's lorries deliver from the nearest concentration depot and load up again with customers' orders. Some buildings are used by light industry; others have been converted into homes. The erstwhile railway houses now usually have other occupants. Old station mills and warehouses may still be used for their original purpose, and a rosebush may still straggle over what remains of the platform; and though the signal-box, once the nerve centre, has long gone, the rhubarb and mint that were part of its occupants' garden are still occasionally harvested. History lies only skin-deep. Even the weeds may tell a story, like those of Australian and South American origin near former mill sidings, sprung from seeds dropped from imported fleeces.

5 The Country Railwayman

Except where they helped develop suburbs on the edges of great cities, railways did not urbanize the countryside but became part of it. The country railwayman was an integral part of this process of naturalization: he belonged to be, just as Hodge and his master; cultivated his garden or plot beside the track, keenly surveyed the progress of other people's crops, often gave a hand at harvest, supplemented his income by setting traps and snares. After he had married a local girl·and their children had entered the village school, he might belong more to the countryside than the railway, and if he changed jobs it could be for a local shop or farm rather than another station.

The village stationmaster was an institution, like schoolmaster, parson or blacksmith. He too might marry a local girl, but he remained foremost a railwayman, often slightly aloof, the district representative of the company – a responsibility that sometimes weighed heavily. If he changed jobs, it would be for promotion along the line. A stationmaster must have worked his way up the ladder, meaning several changes of home and a spell as relief stationmaster, spending a fortnight here and a month there; and on most railways he would be expected to continue applying for better positions as they occurred. So while an unambitious porter or ganger might spend his entire working life in the same cottage doing the same job, becoming only slowly better off as wages rose and working hours reduced, the stationmaster was less permanent, owing allegiance elsewhere, more akin to the Methodist minister.

But he would take part in local affairs and his dress alone ensured he was noticed. 'As I was going forward to the guard's van to identify my trunk and my wooden box,' writes Siegfried Sassoon of his return from school, 'the stationmaster (who, in those days, wore a top-hat and baggy frock coat) saluted me respectfully. Aunt Evelyn always sent him a turkey

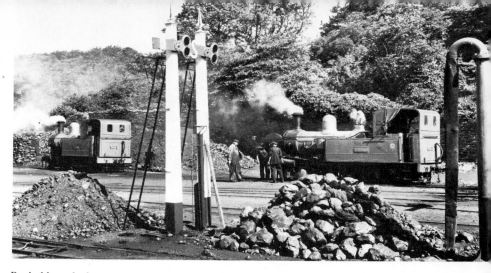

Probably nobody was more committed to his job, living and breathing it round the clock, than the country railwayman, especially the engineman. He might swear about the management, cuss at some awkward design feature in his loco's innards, but he frequently dreaded the thought of his last run and the blankness of retirement to follow. This splendid early morning shot outside the shed at Douglas in the Isle of Man is dedicated to the memory of all enthusiastic railwaymen.

at Christmas.' Socially you would be most likely to mix with him at the pub.

In his *Brensham Village*, John Moore portrays life at the Adam & Eve, the village's railway pub only a hundred yards from the station. 'The stationmaster had his morning and evening pint there, pulling out his great turnip-watch every time a train went by; our only porter spent a good deal of time there, as he could afford to do, since the even tenor of his life was interrupted only by four stopping trains a day; and at noon the gangers came in and ordered pints of cider, sat down in the corner and had their bait.' Here as in railway pubs up and down the country the stationmaster might have little to say to his fellow-railwaymen; he was their superior and inspector. And he was rarely loved by others in the village, having few friends closer than the landlord of the pub where he was often the best customer.

He fleetingly appears in many people's memories as a lonely character, pacing up and down the platform in his rather ridiculous hat,

The village stationmaster and his staff were the first civilians to wear uniform in the countryside.

frightened that something might go wrong. In *The Railway Children*, 'the Station Master concealed himself in the shadow of a brake-van that had a little tin chimney and was labelled "G.N. & S.R. 34576 Return at once to White Heather Siding" and in this concealment he lurked.' To lurk was like the gamekeeper, and he was not a popular figure either.

The stationmaster's chief problem was his classlessness in the highly stratified country society. Though seldom realizing it, he was part of the breaking-down of the old ways of life. Unlike others with responsible jobs in the village or market town, he had risen from the ranks not by any outstanding effort of self-help but through plodding progression. He usually lived 'over the shop' like a vulgar tradesman, and that his shop was often a mile or more from the town centre must have added to his loneliness. His lack of education could handicap him in his job as well as in village society. Had he been a gentleman he might have relaxed with his subordinates and had the confidence to challenge district headquarters when inflexible rules and lack of consultation over timetable changes prevented him increasing his traffic.

Except in their early years, when novelty was all, the railways did not employ gentlemen for any ordinary job. Even by 1840 Branwell Brontë's

70

appointment as assistant clerk at Sowerby Bridge was regarded as a definite declassment. 'I wrote to London to learn what situation a Railway afforded for *Gentlemen* to fill – not knowing before those applications reached me that there were any beside those for the Engineer, Solicitor, and Secretary, and conclude ... that an inspector's situation is not of that description,' writes the promoter of a West Country branch line to a parent worried by his son's lack of career in 1845. And how were engine drivers recruited, asks a writer of the same date. 'Is it not astonishing that whereas the driver of a coach and four horses, value a few hundreds, and say twenty passengers, should have been a man, for the most part, from the middle class, the driver of a railway engine and train, with say one hundred passengers and so many thousands worth of property, should be from the lower orders? It would have astonished anyone to have seen, as I did, the material from which engine drivers sprung.'

They spring of course from cleaners; while middle-class lads might have applied to become engine drivers direct, they would not endure the slow process through cleaner, shunting-engine fireman, goods-engine fireman, slow passenger-engine fireman, and so on. Nor would those who might have enjoyed commanding a small country station in their twenties have submitted first to years of entering up goods received and goods despatched among rows of clerks in the goods offices of even moderately-sized market-town stations.

So we find stationmasters with much poorer education carrying far more responsibility than assistants at the country bank; often they struggled. Only one stationmaster between York and Milford Junction was able to operate the telegraph in 1851, W. W. Tomlinson tells us in his famous *North Eastern Railway*. In 1852 one still 'had not learnt to work the telegraph, or at all events paid no attention to it'. Lack of education and training is a theme repeated throughout the one autobiography of a working country stationmaster, Ernest J. Simmons' *Memoirs of a Station Master*:

Self – 'I have never booked any goods out, sir.'
Mr M. – 'Quite time you learnt to do so then. What did you do in the goods office at Snorum?'
Self – 'Inward goods, sir.'
Mr M. – 'Then, what on earth can be the difference? In one case you receive

an invoice, check the rate, calculate the charge, and enter it in a book; whereas in the other case, you take the consignment note, fix the rate, calculate the charge, and make out the invoice, copying that also. Don't trouble me with such nonsense.'

Self – 'But, sir, I have the ticket booking to do, and I do not know at what rate to charge the things.'

Mr M. – 'Then, sir, refer to the Clearing House Classification, and if the invoices are not properly made out, I shall report the case to Mr Petlum.' Now if Mr Mulberry had said, 'Struggles [Simmons' pseudonym for himself], it is so long since I made out an invoice myself that I have forgotten all about it; I don't want to expose my ignorance to you, therefore I bully,' he would have told the truth. It took me all that night to find out how, and to invoice those goods. The reference to the Railway Clearing House Classification was not quite so easy as one would imagine.

Mulberry, like so many stationmasters, was at constant loggerheads with higher officials and had to rely on his clerk to patch up relationships and get the job done. Earlier we find Struggles working as a booking clerk for stationmaster Milsom at Wilderness Road (a fictitious name for a wayside station between Didcot and Swindon). Milsom received a letter from the district superintendent's office complaining that though the company had equipped the station 'with a telegraph instrument, together with an alphabetical code, etc, neither yourself nor your staff have taken the trouble to learn how to send or how to receive telegraphic messages; and I now beg to inform you that I shall visit your station on the first proximo, and that unless I find that someone is proficient, I shall then report the matter to the Directors, who will probably question your aptitude for the post of stationmaster.'

Simmons' account of what followed throws vivid light on the kind of man who was in charge of the new form of transport:

The dummy telegraph instrument went back, and my London instructor commenced to talk to me on the proper instrument. I was calling for him shortly after this, when my calling was interrupted by some other station, who said:–

'Who are you?'

I replied as well as I could, when I received the following message:

'Tell Milsom to look out for Calcraft; coming down by the 10.30.' ... As Mr Milsom had gone across to the hotel to take an early luncheon I thought

Whatever their job, railwaymen took it seriously and this involved a readiness to pose for the camera by no means always shown by contemporaries in other industries.

73

I had better go and tell him, although I considered it was perhaps only a joke ... To my surprise this information electrified Mr Milsom, and I really began to associate it with the drop scene; his usually flushed face turned quite white, and he quiveringly replied –

'Joke be hanged. You'll live long enough to find that it's no joke. Don't you know that Calcraft is our auditor?'

Since the auditor had only recently paid a visit, the stationmaster had thought it safe to borrow some money from the till, which had quickly to be repaid. Calcraft duly arrived.

'I suppose,' said he, 'you did not expect to see me again quite so soon, but I heard that you had a protege of Mr Butcher's here as booking clerk, and I was anxious to "make his acquaintance".'

Here he poked Mr Milsom in the ribs with one finger, and they both laughed until Mr Calcraft had a violent fit of coughing. When he had recovered from this attack, Mr Milsom looked at his watch, and said something about luncheon.

'Yes, yes,' said Mr Calcraft, 'you know I just like a glass of ale and a crust about eleven o'clock; but don't be in a hurry, Milsom, you know me ... there are a few old friends that I always have to shake hands with, and let us proceed. First of all, there is my old friend in prison, Mr Petty Cash; how is he? Let me shake hands with him ... Next, there are my old friends the train book and the cash book; I mean the daily remittance book. Let me see if they are good friends still ... Now let me look at my old friend, the coal sold book ... Now Milsom, I will go and take luncheon with you, but my motto is "Business first and pleasure after".'

Simmons' memories are often about the dread of visitations from officials on high – and again poor education. At another station years later, an accident happens because the clerk despatching a train could not work the telegraph and had only read half the rule book during his first six months of employment. Life at country stations was not unalloyed bucolic bliss for such men. On being promoted stationmaster himself (incidentally in place of one sacked for inability to keep the accounts straight), Simmons moralizes:

With all due respect to the station masters of the present day, I beg to say that a station master at a small station was then a personage of much greater importance in the estimation of the public than he is now. It was a new thing,

74

and clerks and stationmasters were for the most part supplied from the middle class of society, and able to hold their own in a gentlemanly way; whereas, at the present day, they are, for the most part, descendants of the porters and policemen, who, having been educated at the British and Free Schools, have been drafted into the Telegraph Office, and thence to the clerks' appointments. There is nothing sharpens the wits of a lad like a telegraph office, but it cannot be expected that the associations of their homes will make them conversant with the habits and manners of gentlemen. Consequently when these young men become stationmasters they also become 'Jacks in Office', and have seriously injured the old friendly feeling which existed between the public and the officials.

At the same time there is a considerable amount of importance attached to this public place of meeting – the railway station. The Jones's who don't associate with the Robinsons, meet there. Mr Jones would not like the stationmaster to touch his cap to the Robinsons, and pass him without notice, so he sends the stationmaster a hare. The Rev Mr Silvertongue is always wanting to take a party somewhere at single fare for the double journey, or some other concession, so he honours the stationmaster by conversing with him, as an equivalent for concessions. The old lady with her dog would not, on any account, have the little dear put into that dreadful dungeon of a dog box when she travels, so she sends the stationmaster a basket of plums once in the year ... The grocer and other tradesmen want their claims for delay and damage (by which they hope to extort an additional profit) attended to, so they encourage the stationmaster by standing trade whenever they meet him at the inn; or send him a box of French plums. The doctor hopes to be sent for in case of a railway accident, so he is polite. 'My lord' knows he has no right to bully at the railway station, so he brings a brace of pheasants, and thus adds Mr Station Master to the train of his servants.

Most stationmasters received presents from their leading customers well into this century, often until after the 1939–45 war, tips that almost underline their lonely lot. As one talks to retired country railwaymen, including stationmasters, it stands out that their happiest years were those before they had to look after a station of their own, when they did not have to discipline and spy, were not worried by whether the takings were kept up or whether the signalman was allowing visitors in his box. Of course they took pride in their jobs, recounting compliments received and awards for best-kept stations and gardens; but the pride hung heavily.

'Garrh ... I'll teach they danged so-'n-so's to toot and whistle at me!'

Getting trains away smartly, avoiding even the slightest accident in the goods yard, fighting for more appropriate timetables, ordering enough but not too many cattle wagons for the monthly fair, catching passengers (perhaps the friend of wife or daughter) riding without tickets, balancing the books, keeping the toilets clean and the petunias watered, checking the consumption of oil in the lamps: these were things more to be worried about than enjoyed. Loneliness would be emphasized by poor relations with the district office and rivalry with adjoining stationmasters. 'Don't tell Mr — that there's an inspector coming tomorrow; let him find out for himself.' 'Why can't you get the freight away sooner? You only think of your own convenience.'

In later times many stationmasters were deeply concerned by the disappearance of traffic to the roads. 'When I took over, the bus company had just put on a market-day bus,' one retired stationmaster told me. 'I asked my predecessor what I could do about it. He said "Do about it? There's nothing you can do about it and the less you try the less nuisance you'll be." Well, I was keen in those days and couldn't let it pass and wrote several letters to District Office asking if they'd allow cheap tickets to be sold on market day, but I was wasting my time. The train left at 9.52 and cheap tickets couldn't be issued before 10.'

Much later, in the 1950s, I happened to call at a country station when the stationmaster was raging on the telephone to headquarters. Much of his traffic was meat from an abattoir hitherto without road access, but at that very moment builders were threatening to knock a hole which would allow a lorry to back up to the building, across a rail siding. The stationmaster began by taking the law into his own hands, shunting a couple of trucks to block the builders' way. An abattoir official had then telephoned railway headquarters to demand that the obstruction be removed, and headquarters (without inquiring into the legal position) first told the stationmaster not to make a nuisance of himself.

Especially in these later years stationmasters were often to complain they were mere clerks whose voice carried no weight. A branch with a dozen stations had no one person to represent its interests; each stationmaster reported directly to district headquarters whose staff sincerely wanted a quiet life. The afternoon train might not have been retimed to miss a vital connection, or be too early for workers at the egg factory, had there been a real spokesman. When 'line managers' were first suggested, British Railways said no, each station needed its own resident boss; latterly, area managers have duly taken over.

But whatever the quality of management, railways have always been tied in red tape. The paperwork, even at country stations, was prodigious. The torment of reasonably capable stationmasters unable to balance the monthly accounts was formidable – reports, reports, reports had to be rendered, even though the company's rat catcher (later rodent operator) did turn up to enquire if any rats had been seen, accept a verbal negative and go off on the next train. Instructions from up the line came in a steady year-long bombardment. Stop lamps being thrown up to the roofs of passenger coaches by men with greasy hands, causing smearing; check foot-warmers are in order after their withdrawal from service on 30 April; no longer accept foreign copper or bronze coins in payment of fares; bicycles in store should now be charged 4d for two days; no longer any need to lock passengers in their coaches, but take great care to ensure they don't fall out; milk churn rates amended, 50–75 miles $1\frac{1}{8}$d per imperial gallon; milk churns not being loaded expeditiously enough; swine fever about, so pigs to be refused; market people taking baskets into compartments must be stopped; commercial travellers now travel double trip for single fare at weekends, but document to be signed by their employer and photograph carried; every station must display Explosives Act; and so it goes on. This selection comes from around 1885.

Every week some kind of fare was adjusted: bands of musicians and professional singers: 8 persons or more at fare and a quarter. Engines and horses of firemen attending fire-brigade demonstrations: single rate. Chess-club members now conveyed at Picket Ticket rate. Bona-fide emigrants going third class allowed a hundredweight of luggage. Special luggage allowances for commercial travellers, theatrical parties, equestrian performers and operatic parties, but 1d a mile extra if special vehicle required. Professional swimmers engaged at music halls to give exhibitions of swimming in tanks fixed upon stage to be treated in the same manner as theatrical parties. But of course. Monkeys accompanying organ-grinders to be charged at the same rate as dogs.

Then the stationmaster had to 'ascertain whether the Company are affected, so far as the Rates and Taxes are concerned, by the formation

78

of School Boards, or of Local Boards or Sewerage Districts or by the provision of Water Supply'. Not surprisingly, it was the stationmaster who first employed a typewriter in many country areas. Not surprisingly too, he found what excuse he could to leave his office to see trains off, especially from up platforms – it was Arnold Bennett who described the up platform as the 'modish' one, the pull of London being felt throughout the land, departures being more important than arrivals. He found reason, too, to visit principal customers, such as the quarry which might yield £2,000 a month, more than the rest of the customers put together, and the signalbox.

The signalman in his cabin – Smallbrook Junction, Isle of Wight. Note the single-line token instruments, and the loops in which the tokens were placed to facilitate speedy hand exchanges with drivers.

The signalman in his spotlessly clean domain, its levers polished daily and always pulled with a cloth, was nominally under the stationmaster's authority and had to submit the train register for signature on each sheet. But he was independent, less stressed. At busy times he might be expected to help in the parcels office, but though working a long day he had plenty of time to cook himself a meal, darn his socks, and probably work on the plot within earshot of the block instrument on which the next station asked permission for a train to proceed. 'The signalmen are the elite of the village railwaymen,' said Alfred Williams who worked for the Great Western before becoming poet and author. 'Their wages are better, their work cleaner and brainier – it is genteel by the side of that of the plate-layers and farm-hands – but there is greater responsibility attaching to the post. Good reliable men only are retained in the signalboxes, who have been tried and proved, who are unhampered with exterior business, able to concentrate their whole thought and mind on the signals and in-struments. One lapse of memory would be sufficient to bring about a calamity; they would be ruined as far as their life on the railways is con-cerned.'

In the days before interlocking and other safety devices, many were indeed ruined or demoted to porters. (More recently some failed signal-men have been switched to station announcing.) But the vagaries of headquarters, the pressures to win promotion, could largely pass them by. They generally wore their responsibility lightly, chatted on the phone to their colleagues in neighbouring boxes in a way that stationmasters, even supporting their own dignity and the company's image, seldom did. They waved – and still do – good-humouredly at passing drivers, who might occasionally pass over a lump of coal to augment official rations, exchange newspapers between boxes, or even carry a bottle of cider from another station nearer a pub to a box bereft. 'Strictly no admittance' said the notice on the door, but drivers of goods trains waiting to be overtaken, gangers, perhaps the driver of the station bus and a regular passenger or two, sometimes turned the box into a happy club.

Many signalmen stayed in the same box most of their working life. The true branch-line signalman was paid less than his main-line counter-part but with many fewer trains to handle he could often earn pocket money, rabbiting or repairing bicycles between trains. Since most branch lines closed at night, but signalboxes had to be open from first to last train, he also stood to gain more overtime than men at main-line boxes staffed for continuous service. At branch-line passenger stations he normally collected the tickets, unless 'crossing' trains in the loop on the single track, when in full view of passengers he would demonstrate his importance, running to and fro with the single-line tokens, ringing bells with neighbouring boxes and pulling most of his levers within a few minutes.

The life of the isolated crossing-keeper was different. Whether he had a real box and a large wheel to open and close the gates, or did it by hand having learnt of the train's approach from an instrument in his cottage, he was seldom visited, was outside the railway community. These men had no raison d'être that a bridge would not replace. But there were thousands of them, and still are many, especially in the flatter areas of eastern and north-eastern Britain.

With less onerous jobs, crossing-keepers mainly continued twelve-hour stints after main-line signalmen's hours were shortened to ten in the 1880s and 1890s. This was at first achieved by having five men to service two boxes continuously open, the fifth man undertaking four hours at each box with two hours to walk between them. Before the ten-hour day, many accidents had been put down to tiredness, and even after it there would be dangerously long continuous stretches: at the weekend the late-duty signalman went on to take up his first early turn.

The engine drivers were the railway's little lords, the speeding experts every schoolboy wished to become; where engines were stabled and crews employed, there would always be long waiting-lists of applicants. Priority was given to sons or other close relatives, helping build long family traditions of railway employment. Engine drivers were often men of character, a character you could sometimes tell by hearing or experiencing how they handled their steeds in difficulties. Long periods travelling through the country sharpened their senses for crops and wild life, as they pointed out pheasants and mushrooms to the firemen with whom they sometimes paired for a decade or more. A North Eastern driver was suspended for a fortnight for driving without his fireman whom he had allowed to go picking mushrooms. In early days even smoking on duty could bring dismissal, suspension or fine. Many were surprisingly well read; the driver of a goods train on which I took an unofficial lift asked his fireman to take charge and read several pages of poetry aloud between stations. Large size seemed usual: generally railways liked their men large, and right up to general management, perhaps missing out signalmen, an extra stone seemed to help with promotion. Engine drivers started as cleaners, and even if a mini-railway owned but one locomotive there would still be a lad cleaner who would light up first thing in the morning. Labour was cheap, machinery dear, so it was foolish not to provide generous manpower. Even a train of five four-wheeled coaches on the branch line of 1850–90 would have two guards.

At the start each driver and fireman had their own engine, locked up in their off-duty hours. On a line with but one machine, thirteen- or fourteen-hour days could thus be the rule, becoming eighteen if a connecting main-line train was late through bad weather. But steadily rotas were introduced, men changing machines often at remote stations halfway down a branch line and halfway through their working day. The 'roster' might be different for each week of the year.

Enginemen were always among the best paid, and for over a century were the most militant. An early union, the Engine Drivers' & Firemen's United Society, was behind the 1867 pressure for a minimum wage of 5s 6d per day for drivers, rising to 7s 6d after six years, with 3s 6d rising to 4s 6d for firemen – note the differential; a ten-hour day and six-day guaranteed week, time and a half on Sundays, a new top coat once a year, a lodging allowance of 2s 6d for nights away from home, an hour to prepare and stable at the beginning and end of the day, and free passes for man and family, were demanded. Five major companies conceded most of this, but not the North Eastern which sacked 1,080 strikers, including many based at country depots. Only 241 were ever re-employed, as the long waiting-lists of would-be enginemen could be exploited. Strikers on the Brighton line were imprisoned, and that ended the union.

It also ended the era when the country railwayman was better paid than his neighbours working on the land and in quarries and local industries. Even *The Times*, though making piously plain it did not condone strikes, felt constrained to point out in 1871 that 'a great part of the excessive labour exacted from railway servants might have been avoided or mitigated if railway servants, like other skilled workmen, had known how to combine.' The story of railway unions is long and complicated, leading to the first national railway strike in 1911. Union members right up and down the country obeyed the call, country and town railwaymen standing together. And they won.

For the record, the ten-hour day was nearly universal by 1874, though branch-line drivers still received only a basic 6s a day, firemen 3s 4d, in 1883. In 1907 the overall average railway wage was 25s 10d, and more than the proportional number of country railwaymen were among the two-fifths (or 100,000 men) earning less than 20s. Rowntree of York then thought the poverty-line for a family with three children was 21s 8d. Railwaymen had truly slid down the social scale, as they continued to do. But the branch line still offered interest, pride, security. In 1927, the national wage was claimed by the unions to be 72s to 90s for drivers working 48 hours, and in 1958 was 198s (£9.90) to 222s (£11.10) for 44 hours.

Gangers and platelayers were the rugged, hard-drinking railway staff. Out in the elements even more than farm labourers, they knew and explored the potential of every inch of the 'road' under their charge and every corner of the fields and woods each side. Judicious poaching was everyday, but in the mid-nineteenth century with wages at 16s a week they sold their catch, rather than bring the luxury of meat to their own table; the fare they carried to their remote lineside huts was of the plainest. They had the highest accident rate among railwaymen, and on scarcely a mile of track in Britain has a ganger not been run down by

Gangers, the rugged, hard-drinking railway staff. This group comes from Devon.

an unexpected train or light engine, its approach often drowned by a gale. In *Brensham Village* we meet a ganger whose partner had been killed by an express.

At the age of fifty-five he was earning a little more than two pounds a week, and would have thought himself comfortably off but for the shadow of old age which lay ahead of him. He'd never been able to save anything; and the company which he had served so long and faithfully provided no pensions for their servants in the lower grades when they were worn out and old. So David couldn't have retired even if he'd wanted to; and he patiently carried on as he'd done ever since he was promoted from platelayer to ganger, 'walking his stretch' every day and in all weathers, on Sundays as well as weekdays, for rather less than fifty shillings. His back became more bent and his legs more stiff from treading the sleepers; but his sharp eyes that could see a rabbit-track in the cutting forty yards away still kept faithful watching along the road for the rot in the timber or the fault in the steel, for the wet patch in the clay or the displaced brick in the culvert or the tell-tale seeping of sand from a crack in the embankment.

Whatever his job and background, a railwayman was always a railwayman. Miners and quarrymen who became engine drivers and fitters, soldiers finishing a tour of duty, promising young lads, and shop and innkeepers ending their independence who took up clerical jobs, village labourers and craftsmen who filled vacancies for porters and platelayers,

Railwaymen were often the first people to use new processes and machines in their community, but in the second half of the twentieth century had to continue with archaic processes such as hanging oil lamps and turning on gas ones by hand – still done at many country stations – and (see facing page) turning locomotives by muscle power. To be fair, this ex-Great Eastern 0-6-0 which had brought the daily goods to Wells Next the Sea in Norfolk in May 1961 was deputizing for a sick diesel-electric and the turntable was stiffer than it had been in its prime.

they all quickly shared a common tradition of pride and service, battling against unnecessarily blunt central management. The uniform worn by most ranks played an important part; hitherto only soldiers had appeared in uniform in most villages. Discipline was also important. Early travellers were pleasantly surprised by the courtesy of railwaymen, the absence of badgering for tips. So even the farm labourer who had doubled his earnings as porter, and who would have gone back to the land in preference to being moved out of his native village, was still fully a railwayman, part of that great steam communication system that not only linked every part of the country but was a great civilizing force in its own right, teaching its staff safety, cleanliness, the value of pretty gardens, offering them and their families cheap travel, insurance and much else. And once a railwayman, much of the tradition stuck; those (relatively few) who returned to earlier jobs tended to keep in touch with former colleagues, while the retired constantly returned to their station or depot even in the days before there was a pension to collect. The conversation was bound to involve gardening, for railwaymen were always keen gardeners, perhaps because most worked on a shift basis and even in winter had free daylight hours to work on their own plots or do jobbing for someone else.

6 The Country Train

If the distinction was not always clear between a country railway and a railway running through the countryside, the country train stood out clearly from the express which passed so anonymously through its territory. Country trains were short, usually of only four or five old coaches, sometimes one. Four-wheelers were still used on many services in the 1920s, long after bogie vehicles were standard on main lines. Clerestory coaches, those with a raised central section of roof to give better ventilation, also survived in rural backwaters after disappearing elsewhere. True, some railways had purpose-built country trains, perhaps labelled Such-and-Such Branch Train No. One; but these were exceptions. Generally the country made do with what inter-urban services had outgrown.

The locomotives could vary from powerful machines of yesteryear working a gentle retirement, to varieties of the ubiquitous 0-6-0 tank, whose replica was to be found on most toy railways. Few country trains had named locomotives, though older readers will remember those rural names like *Chaffinch* and *Pershore Plum* given by the Great Western to its 4-4-0 'Bulldog' class, introduced in 1898 and surviving till nationalization half a century later. The 'Bulldogs' followed the 'Dukes', and when the GW needed more machines of similar capabilities for the Cambrian services in mid-Wales, it cannibalized some of the then-30-year-old 'Bulldogs', creating 'Dukedogs' which did all that was expected of them. Continuity on the branch line was especially strong in the West of England and Wales, since the Great Western was the only railway to retain its identity at the Grouping of companies in 1923. The dark green of its locomotives and the chocolate and cream of its coaches had originated in the broad gauge.

Elsewhere 1923 spelt gradual standardization, though many pre-grouping engines in new colours continued to work until nationalization and beyond, the 4-4-0 'Skye bogies' of the Highland Railway, for instance, which started their life, to quote O. S. Nock, in the 'gay music-hall style of the Victorian Highland painting, and continued through the era of dark, plain unlined green, survived to bear the alien Midland "red" after grouping in 1923, and to look extraordinarily well in it'. Most of us today never saw the Brighton yellow 4-4-0 tanks with tall copper-

The Victorian country train. LSWR 0-6-2ST at Fort Brockhurst with a Lee-on-the-Solent train; and a mixed train near Castle Douglas on the troubled Portpatrick & Wigtownshire during the period the Caledonian operated it.

capped chimneys and names in gilt letters the full length of their tanks, or the yellow-green 2-2-0s with a large single driver and an underframe and tender painted in medium chocolate, the Great Northern's Patrick Stirling's inspiration, haul a local out of Boston. The trains once had as much variety as the country stations they served; there was still character enough to please a demanding enthusiast during the 1939–45 war and immediately after.

In Victoria's reign the merchandise on most branch lines travelled in strings of trucks behind the passenger coaches; the erratic progress of these mixed trains had to depend on the prosperity of trade and the season of the year. *Punch* and more solemn travel critics warned against the idiosyncracies of the mixed train, clearly identified in most company timetables. Although – except on light railways and the narrow gauge – freight was later marshalled into separate trains, until the 1940s and the early 1950s the passenger ensemble might still include an odd van or two, a cattle or milk truck and a horse box – what the railways called coaching traffic, harking back to the days when the well-to-do took their coach with them. Early timetables also indicated which trains allowed that (or more usually which expresses did not).

No confident displaying in the main platforms at large city and junction stations for the country train: it would be tucked discreetly into some terminal bay. The whole thing revealed at a glance that it would only come to life in its own good time and would amble along at an average speed rarely exceeding 20 mph or so including frequent stops and occasional total cessations to replenish its water tanks. One has to admit that some not strictly rural services shared some of these characteristics, but the country train could also be readily identified by its cargo – human and goods.

Passengers represented the full cross-section of the community in a way not shared by expresses, which until after the 1939–45 war catered mainly for the select going on long journeys. Some used the country train as the first or last stage of a longer journey and came with conventional railway luggage – case upon case stowed in the van, hatbox and picnic hamper in the compartment. Most were on local journeys, about their everyday business; some never travelled on any train but that running through their own valley. Few would visit even half the places in the pictures hung under the luggage racks, even though all these were of places served by the same railway. They carried their shopping, the produce of garden and allotment being taken to friends and relatives or for sale in the market, a piece of household equipment, tools, new clothes.

Schedules often allowed time to add or detach a horse box or cattle wagon and for gossip at the station. This was where the railway had its roots, where passengers and staff, often related, shared the same few shops and interests, where the passage of the trains told labourers in the fields what o'clock it was, where the guard beamed with genial importance as he handed out perambulators or bicycles and passed the stationmaster his pouch or water-can from the next station.

Although all branch-line trains were slow, and most of them old, their character reflected the length of route and whether there was any through traffic. The shortest lines, like Yatton & Clevedon in Somerset, or the Killin Railway after the abandonment of steamers on Loch Tay from a lochside station, had no stopping place except junction and terminus and connected towns inconveniently bypassed by the main line. One engine and coach could suffice. Dozens of longer branches were also self-contained, ranging from the Dingwall–Kyle of Lochalsh (63 miles) across the whole width of Scotland, and the famous Royal Deeside line (43 miles), on whose excursions passengers were with typical Granite City frugality packed into one compartment at a time, a new one not being unlocked till officials were satisfied every seat had been taken, children placed on laps, to the Newport–Freshwater (21 miles), a genuine branch on the Isle of Wight.

On branches running between two junction towns few passengers might be making through journeys; the Gloucester to Hereford line with its junction at Ross-on-Wye for the Wye Valley branch was one, and little systems of branches vied with one another to offer through passengers the slowest transit. All three routes from Aberdeen to Inverness were excruciatingly slow. Finally there were lines with claims to be through trunk routes but so little traffic that they had to be operated on the branch principle, their rare trains stopping everywhere; to travel from Chelten-ham to Southampton on the Midland & South Western Junction was a sore trial of patience. Some of these lines, such as the Somerset & Dorset,

The place is Charlestown on the north bank of the Forth near Rosyth, the time a bright winter's morning in 1962. The locomotive is of the basic 0-6-0 type that eased goods trains to the water's edge at countless sea and inland harbours throughout the British Isles, for before the days of centralization and containers the country harbour was as important as the country railway. No. 65323 had

the honour of travelling on an ancient route; it was as early as 1767 that the Charlestown Railway was opened, its wagons occasionally carrying passengers to join the Granton–Sterling packet boats. Up to 23,000 people a year used these pre-steam railway 'boat trains'.

with its famous Manchester–Bournemouth *Pines Express*, had occasional services calling only at the most important towns; but most remained all-station trains, their wheels firmly bogged in the countryside. So in 1910, the 1.50 from Bournemouth West did not descend from the Mendips into Bath, 71 miles away, until 6.0, and perhaps with a similar 4-4-0 tender engine, though in different livery, the Midland & Great Northern prolonged the agony of getting over the 96 flat miles from Doncaster to March from 2.10 until 6.18 – with the compensation of a chance to stretch the legs and get refreshed for a few minutes at Lincoln.

In much of Ireland the all-station train was the only way of making real journeys as well as going to market or travelling from one village to the next; short-distance travellers, though continually changing, usually outnumbered those going the whole way. Scotland, though in the forefront of express and express locomotive development for services between its main cities and England, could incarcerate you particularly uncomfortably. The line all the way from Inverness to Wick, 161 miles, was but a glorified branch, and in 1910, when the trip took seven hours, the Highland Railway could still carry you in vehicles built in the 1870s: five compartments each accommodating ten people in a truck 25 feet long and 7 feet wide, a weight-passenger ratio of about a quarter that provided by British Rail standard stock.

The atmosphere was easier than on trains connecting different parts of the country. Many of the passengers, relaxed, on familiar ground, knew each other and commented freely on the state of the crops, criticized the construction of hayricks. Even the guard looked his part, less earnest, perhaps a shade shabbier, carnation or rose in his buttonhole, happier and freer than his better-paid express counterpart keeping up with double-home working and such complications.

Passengers and pace varied according to time of day and season, with rushes as children went to school and returned in the afternoon, more people and a festive mood on market days, less travel and more tension as harvest time approached, especially if the weather was bad, special noisy roistering on that institution the Saturday-night extra. Right down to the 1950s, probably half Britain's branch lines closed later on Saturdays, gangs of teenage boys, courting couples, perfume and fish and chips percolating into the scene. A happy passenger with uncertain gait would

'Zorry about that there Lunnon connection o' yours, zir, but we can't disturb old Annie 'ere – often as not she lays a double-yolker.'

The Great Western stopping train. Though the exact class of locomotive might vary, they all belonged to the same basic family with their distinct tapering boilers. Journeys from one part of the West of England to another might involve using four or five such trains in succession. This picture was taken on the Gloucester–Hereford line.

arrive from the nearest hostelry just before departure time and produce a roar as he asked the guard if he knew where he was going and did he require any help.

The guard's van on a country train would include everything, not always forgetting the kitchen sink. As well as the passengers' belongings there would be bottled gas, empty flower, fish and poultry boxes being returned to their owners, pigs and day-old chicks, pigeons (always being consigned everywhere as a kind of national pastime – said to have helped us win the wars[1]), seed potatoes, bags and parcels from a national food or other manufacturer to be cast off in twos and threes at stations along the line, mailbags, the railway's own registered letters and parcels, the pouch in which the stationmaster sent his daily takings and received weary

1. In 1976, British Rail stunned fanciers by announcing that unaccompanied livestock, including pigeons, were uneconomic and would no longer be carried.

official communications, boxes of glass, trees and shrubs, bins of ice cream. Return trips would bring back the produce of the countryside, including growers' specialities such as watercress, asparagus and mushrooms, calves to be exchanged with farmers elsewhere as genetic standards rose (nor should we forget the benefit to rural human genetics brought by the railway: with less inter-marrying the 'village idiot' has disappeared), and – until centralized creameries arrived – milk, butter and cheese. Not cream, for that would not keep long enough for railway handling in pre-pasteurized days and hence was a purely local dish.

Almost wherever you went in rural Britain, the local railway mixture was similar: relaxed though purposeful, permeated by the smell of the land to which it belonged.

The country train usually left a big station or junction a few minutes after the departure of an express – not just to give passengers a convenient connection but to use track capacity. If a local stopping at mainline wayside stations was sent off sharply in the wake of one express, it could make a dash – relatively speaking – to the next traffic centre ahead of the following one. On true branch lines the pace was less hurried; and on hilly roads, when the engine was not struggling to regain speed uphill after a stop at the valley bottom, it was being steadied for a speed restriction downhill or across the next bridge or viaduct. Not that lines in flat areas were faster: the Great Eastern's in East Anglia managed to be among the slowest.

The most rural of rural trains of course began not from a junction with the main line but from one deep in the country between branches, places like Maud Junction for Fraserborough or Peterhead, and Moat Lane Junction and Talyllyn Junction on the same route to Brecon, itself served by four branch-line services, all stopping at all stations. The senior branch line's train which had slipped humbly out of a bay platform at the city station now had the dominant role, arriving at the main platform; the train serving the branch off the branch discreetly waited on the side for a share of passengers and luggage, as at Dulverton, Heathfield, Yelverton to quote three individualistic West Country branch-line junctions. At Yelverton the junior partner was the line to Princetown, highest point on the GW, reached by a serpentine course over the deserted moor. Based at Princetown, its train staff were a rugged group who never came nearer

WEST-END OFFICE—30, Regent Street, Piccadilly Circus.	SOUTH WESTERN RAILWAY. CENTRAL OFFICE—9, Grand Hotel Building, Charing Cross. BOROUGH OFFICE—186, High Street, Borough.	CITY OFFICE— Exeter Building, Arthur Street West, London Bridge.

PROGRAMME OF CHEAP TICKETS
AND GENERAL EXCURSION ARRANGEMENTS FOR
JUNE, 1884.

NOTICE.—These arrangements may be changed or varied from time to time as regards Fares and Times of Trains and Coaches without further announcement, and this Bill holds good only until further notice.

CHEAP FAST EXCURSION TO THE
WEST OF ENGLAND, South and North Devon, Holsworthy (for Bude),
Tavistock, Plymouth, Devonport, Barnstaple, Ilfracombe, Bideford.

On Every SATURDAY until further notice,

A Special Fast Excursion Train will leave Waterloo 8.15 a.m., Shaftesbury Road at 7.28 a.m., Hammersmith (The Grove) at 7.30 a.m., Shepherd's Bush at 7.33 a.m., Kensington 8.10 a.m., West Brompton 8.13, and Chelsea 8.15 a.m. Calling at Vauxhall at 8.20, Queen's Road 7.53, Clapham Junction. 8.25, Wimbledon at 8.32, Surbiton, 8.51, Woking, 9.15 and Basingstoke 9 55 a.m. to take up Passengers for Templecombe, Wincanton, Glastonbury, Wells, Burnham, Shepton Mallet, Radstock, Bath, Yeovil Junction, Yeovil, &c., Exeter, Exmouth Branch, St. Cyres, Crediton, Yeoford, Bow, North Tawton, Sampford Courtenay, Okehampton, Hatherleigh, Ashbury and Northlew, Halwill and Beaworthy, Dunsland Cross, Holsworthy, Bude, Bridestowe, Lidford, Launceston, Cameford, Wadebridge, Tavistock, Gunnislake, Callington and Liskeard, Horrabridge, Bickleigh, Marsh Mills, Mutley, Plymouth North Road, Devonport Coppleston, Morchard Road, Lapford, Eggesford, South Molton Road, Barnstaple, Wrafton, Braunton Morthoe, Ilfracombe, Portsmouth Arms, Umberleigh, Chapelton, Fremington, Instow, Bideford and Torrington.

And an Excursion Train will leave Waterloo Bridge Station at 8.45 a.m.
From Shaftesbury Road 7.28, Hammersmith (The Grove) 8.10, and Shepherd's Bush 7.33, Kensington 8.29, West Brompton 8.32, Chelsea 8.34 a.m.,

Calling at Vauxhall at 8.52 a.m., Queen's Road 8.35 a.m., Clapham Junction at 9.0 a.m., Wimbledon at 9.9 a.m., Surbiton at 9.26 a.m., Weybridge at 9.37 a.m., Woking at 9 46 a.m., Farnboro' at 10.0 a.m., and Basingstoke at 10.30 a.m., to take up passengers for Andover, Salisbury, Wilton, Dinton, Tisbury, Semley (for Shaftesbury), Gillingham, Milborne Port, Sherborne, Sutton Bingham, Crewkerne, Chard Junction, Chard, Axminster (for Lyme Regis and Charmouth), Seaton Junction, Seaton Branch, Honiton, Sidmouth Junction, Sidmouth Branch, Whimple and Broadclyst.

RETURNING ON THE MONDAY WEEK OR MONDAY FORTNIGHT FOLLOWING.
SEE TIME TABLE BELOW.

The Railway from Exeter to Barnstaple, Bideford and Ilfracombe passes through some of the finest scenery in Devonshire, and opens up to the Public the favourite watering places of Ilfracombe, Lynton, Westward Ho! Bude, &c. Exmouth, Sidmouth and Seaton are also favourite watering places.

The New Route to Plymouth and Devonport, via Tavistock, passes through lovely Scenery.

FARES THERE AND BACK.   FARES THERE AND BACK.   FARES THERE AND BACK.

STATIONS. See Note A below. To	1st Cl. s. d.	3rd Cl. s. d.	STATIONS. See Note A below. To	1st Cl. s. d.	3rd Cl. s. d.	STATIONS. See Note A below. To	1st Cl. s. d.	3rd Cl. s. d.
Andover	10 0	6 0	Milborne Port	17 0	10 6	Chapelton	32 6	18 0
Ludgershall	12 0	6 0	Sherborne	18 6	10 6	Barnstaple (for Lynton)		
Collingbourne			Yeovil			Wrafton and Brannton	32 6	19 0
Grafton			Yeovil Junction	20 0	11 0	Ilfracombe and Morthoe	33 0	20 0
Savernake	14 0	7 0	Sutton Bingham			Fremington	32 6	18 6
Marlborough			Crewkerne	21 0	11 6	Instow	32 6	19 0
Ogbourne			Chard Junction	22 0	12 0	Bideford (for Westw'd Ho!)	32 6	19 0
Chiseldon	16 0	8 0	Chard	22 0	12 6	Torrington	33 0	20 0
Swindon Town			Axminster (for Lyme Charmouth)	23 0	12 6	Bow	29 6	15 0
Cirencester	18 0	9 0	Lyme Regis	26 0	15 6	North Tawton		
Salisbury	12 6	7 6	Seaton Junction	24 0	13 0	Sampford Courtenay	30 0	16 6
Wilton	13 0	7 6	Colyton			Okehampton		
Dinton	14 0	8 0	Colyford			Hatherleigh (by ch. from		
Tisbury	14 6	8 6	Seaton	24 6	13 6	Okehampton) B		21 6
Semley	15 0	9 0	Honiton			Ashbury and North Lew	31 0	17 6
Gillingham	15 6	9 6	Sidmouth Junction	25 0	13 6	Halwill and Beaworthy	32 0	18 0
Templecombe Junc. with S. & D.	16 0	10 0	Ottery St. Mary	25 6	14 0	Dunsland Cross	32 6	18 6
Burnham	21 6	12 6	Tipton St. John's	25 6	14 0	Holsworthy	33 0	19 6
Highbridge			Sidmouth	26 0	15 0	Bude (by ch. fm. H'worthy) B	40 0	24 6
Shapwick	21 0	12 0	Whimple	26 0	14 0	Bridestowe		
Glastonbury			Broadclyst	26 6	14 6	Lidford (for Launceston)	32 0	18 0
Wells			Exeter	27 6	15 0	Camelford (By coach	42 0	26 0
West Pennard	20 0	10 0	Topsham			Wadebridge (from		
Pylle			Woodbury Road			Padstow) L'nceston. B	47 6	29 0
Evercreech			Lympstone	28 0	15 6	Tavistock	35 0	21 0
Shepton Mallet			Exm'th (for Budleigh Salterton)			Gunnislake) By Coach	36 0	22 0
Masbury			St. Cyres			Callington) from	37 0	22 0
Binegar			Crediton			Liskeard) Tavistock	39 0	23 0
Chilcompton			Yeoford	28 6	15 6	Horrabridge		
Midsomer Norton			Chagford (by ch. fm. Yeoford) B	81 6	18 6	Bickleigh		
Radstock	20 0	10 0	Copplestone	29 0	16 0	Marsh Mills	35 0	21 0
Wellow			Morchard Road	30 0	16 6	Mutley		
Midford			Lapford	30 0	16 6	Plymouth (North Road)		
Bath (Mid. Stn.)			Eggesford	30 6	17 0	Devonport		
Cole			South Molton Road					
Wincanton			Portsmouth Arms	32 0	17 6			
Henstridge			Umberleigh					
Stalbridge								
Sturminster Newton								
Shillingstone								
Blandford	21 0	12 0						
Spettisbury								
Bailey Gate								

(left margin, vertical) Stations on Somerset and Dorset Railway

A By payment of 20 per cent. on the above fares Passengers will be allowed to return by the two last ordinary Trains on the following Saturday or Saturday week, by the first ordinary Train on the following Sunday, Sunday week or Sunday fortnight.
B Coach Passengers will return by the Trains with which the Coaches run in connection.
Children under Three years of Age, Free. Three to Twelve years, Half-fares. Only one article of Luggage allowed to each Adult Passenger.
The Tickets are not Transferable; are available only at the Stations named upon them, and only by the Excursion Trains there and back.

It displayed express headlamps but stopped almost everywhere and did not rush between stations. On the coastal route between Aberdeen and Inverness near Tillynaught. Ex-Caledonian 4-6-0 '191' class.

to civilization than momentarily at Yelverton, one of a number of stations where the locomotive changed ends of its train by running into a siding and allowing the coaches (often a solitary coach) to slide past it by gravity.

Swapping the engine from one end of its train to the other every time it reached terminus and junction was time-consuming and costly, though an interlude enjoyed by railway lovers who would revel in the finer points of the process; at Bodmin Road, I recall how the 2-6-2 Prairie tank of the Wadebridge train always seemed able to run round smartly while the main-line service with which it connected was in the platform, the three shrill blasts from its whistle to say it had cleared the points echoing through the wooded valley. Trains that could be driven from either end without unhitching the locomotive would be an obvious economy and first appeared as steam railcars, such as the Sentinels, with the engine incorporated in the passenger-carrying vehicle. For various reasons they were not successful and none of the railways that introduced them from around the turn of the century kept them for long. Since they had to

A tempting range of offers in a London & South Western notice. Note the references to the scenery en route.

A Sentinel railcar at Hessle near Hull.

Push-pull or auto-trains were used by most railways and survived even in the Home Counties well after nationalization. Here a Three Bridges to East Grinstead train is being propelled out of Grange Road.

be stabled at locomotive depots, they tended to be dirty – and their usually temperamental engines could create unwelcome black clouds.

Then came the auto-train, retaining the basic economy though with a separate engine, its regulator, brake and other controls repeated in a driving compartment in the passenger vehicle. All the major railways made some use of these push-pull auto-trains, auto-cars, or just cars as several generations of travellers called them, the Great Western having the most, employing them on many of its picturesque routes such as Wye Valley, Exe Valley and beside the Fowey estuary to Quiller-Couch's Troy Town.

Even within the Great Western various models of auto-cars were used, some indeed being built by the Western Region after nationalization, but all had distinctive large windows, with deep ventilators over them, bow ends and, unusual in their day, open accommodation instead of compartments. Part of the ritual of travelling by country train was to see and hear one's fellows airing their preoccupations of the moment, listen to the guard calling out the stations as he slid back the doors on either side of the centre gangway or shouted in ecstasy that a field was plastered with mushrooms. Auto-trains were one class only; you chose the best seat and if Lord Whatsit came after you he would take second choice – which seemed unusual then. Most cars had a slatted floor down the central gangway, not for muddy rural shoes but for better foothold, for like the London tube train today, the auto-car had partly longitudinal seating with a large central corridor for standing passengers. On the road these cars made a rhythm unlike that of ordinary trains, their motion and the dancing of the leather hanging-straps varying as the engine pushed or pulled. At busy times the locomotive might be sandwiched between cars, both pushing and pulling.

A recall auto-car journeys on the GW with neat green locomotives of the 0-4-2 1400 class, including a circuit Trowbury–Patney and Chirton–Westbury–Trowbridge–Melksham on which we never had more than a dozen passengers, on Scotland's only auto-train between Fraserborough and St Combs with fishermen preparing to put to sea among the passengers and the engine-driver's wife handing his tea as the train passed the bottom of the garden, and on two former London & South Western cars with iron gates to prevent people alighting prematurely still used in the 1950s on a Gunnislake–Plymouth service; this was the successor to a train which before Devonport Dockyard had electric light would run at slightly different times each week in spring and autumn as the working day lengthened and shortened.

Contrasts in diesel cars. One of the GWR's pioneer streamlined cars near Limpley Stoke in Somerset in 1936 and one of the early British Railway trains that temporarily improved the economics on the Penrith–Workington line seen here at Bassenthwaite Lake.

Push-pull trains were the precursors of diesel cars, and again it was the Great Western that pioneered these on any scale in Great Britain, a fleet of 38 being introduced in the years after 1934. But though the diesel offered obvious branch-line advantages, quick turnrounds, one man less in the crew and a saving of fuel if not required for a couple of hours between services in the middle of the day, and though many experts energetically stressed their desirability, after nationalization in 1948 British Railways went on to build 1,000 steam locomotives of which, incredibly, many were especially for branch passenger services. On the roads, fewer than 3,000,000 cars were then licensed in Great Britain, compared with over 13,000,000 by 1974. By the time diesel cars or multiple units for the country began appearing in quantity in the early 1960s, it was too late to rescue many services – and having been deprived of the lead in dieselization that they merited, branch lines then had to compete for resources with the main lines, greedy for diesels since steam was to be abandoned. And while the full-scale diesel cars that could also be used on suburban services were reliable, the same could not be said for any of the five types of special light-weight railbuses introduced in the late 1950s for branch-line use. Their chapter of woe (would you, would you not, be able to engage the gear next time?) was short and expensive.

In fact diesels did halt the decline on many routes, especially in the Lake District where they arrived early, and the North East where they were skilfully deployed and promoted. Passengers liked their cleanliness (we forget the dirt of yesterday's railway journeys, the filthy state of LMS and later London Midland Region steam-hauled branch trains, inside and out), the seating arrangements, the view of the track or viaduct through the glass cage where the driver sat. Both railway and scenic enthusiasts came for a new look at the mountain road from Barnard Castle to Penrith, and the coast line from Scarborough by Robin Hood's Bay to Whitby. But true local passengers continued to melt away, often encouraged to buy their own transport by the frequent timetable changes that 'rationalization' was producing; railway lovers and sightseers came to predominate, some lines becoming living museums. The granddaughter of a farmer who had dreaded having to catch his first train, as many country people had, might now take a weekly trip on her local branch while she still could for sheer relaxation. Once all fifteen of us travelling to the little fishing port of Lossiemouth, in time past terminus of a sleeping-car from London, turned out to be what officials despairingly called 'enthusiasts'.

The enthusiast's nostalgia may be forgiven. Whereas today's old men could have seen, say, the same 0-6-0 goods tender engine performing the same shunting movements at precisely the same time of day at Redbrook-on-Wye over a span of half a century, most branch lines have now gone in Britain. But the memories survive, readily refreshed by a glimpse of an abandoned embankment or a branch-line smell. Memories of special occasions, which punctuated the lives of most lines, excursions from the 1840s onward (many country lines sent their contingents of working people to the Great Exhibition of 1851) and, as recently as the late 1950s, of packed special trains carrying children to see the Queen at Barnstaple on four routes; of Sunday-school outings and other holiday specials, a few even bringing restaurant-cars to branch-line stations, like

The diesels were especially welcome when replacing the dirtier variety of country train such as this former Great Eastern outfit plying to Thaxted under British Railways' aegis in 1952.

These two cross-country trains carrying the only restaurant-car of the day along routes served mainly by all-stations stoppers would have attracted many a glance. Top, an Ivo Peters portrait of the Somerset & Dorset's Pines Express en route to Bournemouth, running through the Wellow Valley (locomotives Nos. 40569 and 73049). Bottom, the Brighton–Plymouth train at speed near Newton St Cyres in charge of one of the loveliest of country train locomotives, a superheated T9 of the London & South Western.

a regular Newcastle Sunday excursion to Keswick; of fair days when the lengthened trains would be packed with local families and it would take a quarter of an hour to get 500 people off the platform at Bellingham. There were times when main-line sets of coaches had to be pressed into branch-line service to carry, for example, 12,000 Plymouth people to moorland stations and halts on a bank holiday. Before the car, people went where the train took them, and inland beauty spots had greater importance in summer itineraries. Some of the cafés and other facilities they used here and elsewhere closed with the stations.

All but the least significant country branches had their extra goods trains. Cattle and sheep specials attended markets and fairs, and elaborate arrangements were necessary to carry exhibits in the days when agricultural shows changed locations each year. Turkey specials came up from Norfolk before Christmas, a procession of broccoli trains left Cornwall in good seasons, and a regular Friday night butchers' train ran from Perth market to the Fife coast, small town and village butchers going to their local station in the early hours of Saturday to collect supplies to fulfil weekend orders. Even medium-sized market towns might be visited by a theatre group whose special would be loaded after the last house on Saturday; and circus trains operated until well after the 1939–45 war.

There were days when branch lines (like the Teign Valley) were suddenly pressed into service as diversionary routes for expresses, a main route being blocked (as by the sea at Dawlish). On real as well as model railways, extra traffic adds spice. On branch lines it usually showed how seriously under-used the resources normally were.

The break-down train on its way to a mishap further down the line was one of a number of the railway's own domestic specials that occasionally helped justify the existence of all those signalboxes. Ballast trains appeared with greater regularity, signalmen warning the crews not to stop to pick flowers when dropping their load in mid-section since a regular train was behind. Track re-laying has always been a Sunday occupation, earning valuable overtime, the engineer's special waking up signalboxes that otherwise slept from the passing of the Saturdays-only late passenger to the early goods on Monday morning. In later years the weedkilling train was an annual visitor, while the divisional manager or engineer might take a luxurious look at the route in the inspection saloon: complete with mini-kitchen this provided the best of all ways for a privileged guest to see the country.

Both wars produced their own special occasions. In 1914–18 heavy supply trains followed each other in quick succession to the furthest north of Scotland with materials for Scapa Flow as a kind of pre-oil-age exercise. In 1939–45 most branches received contingents of scared evacuees from London, many of them taking their first glimpse of the countryside. One Devon stationmaster broke the blackout with a big display of oil lamps, believing the risk of enemy attack was nothing to the danger of children falling down the embankment from a train longer than the platform. Byways such as that from Didcot and Newbury to Southampton achieved special status in the build-up to D-day; loop lines were lengthened, but inexperienced signalmen and women could still weave traffic into almost unsortable tangles.

Such pressure could produce even more minor derailments than normally expected on branch lines. At stations approached by steep gradients catch or safety points were provided to derail escaping wagons rather than have them run right away: and derailed they were, sometimes through a train of loose-coupled wagons bouncing back too far, sometimes by a signalman trapping a wagon passing over a point by moving the lever at the wrong moment. Scarcely a station of any size did not at some time smash up the odd goods wagon or two during shunting or setting back to allow a passenger train to overtake. In proper form, everyone would blame everyone else; the driver saw the signals as green, the signalman knew they were red; the driver saw the track spread before his very eyes, the platelayer had checked the accuracy of the gauge that very morning. Such incidents might lead to high tension among station communities and to announcements like 'The train to Aberystwyth is the bus standing outside the station', but they involved no risk to passengers. The safety record for country passengers was remarkable, though in the early days before the single-line token or staff system was perfected there was always a chance of head-on collision, in a lonely spot away from help, between two trains incorrectly allowed into the section at the same time. The last head-on crash on a country railway was at Abermule on the Cambrian in 1921, long after the system was technically foolproof. A classic account by L. T. C. Rolt is included as appendix partly for the light it sheds on daily working conditions among a small team of remote railwaymen whose laxness sent colleagues and passengers to their death.

Finally, one recalls the guards, the captains of ships swaying through the countryside, whose appearance, speech, superstitions, even in the 1950s sometimes seemed more Dickensian than twentieth century. The guard who discovering a door swinging open shouted into the night: 'I see you! Where are you? If I get you, you'll be the sorrier for it. Come quickly or you'll be sorry. I know you're not there at all. Stop fooling me. It's I who didn't catch the door. Blast you!'

7 South Molton

A three-coach train came briskly to a standstill, provoking a porter to find his cap and stroll from the parcels office: 'South Molton, South Molton!'

The signalman exchanged the single-line token with the driver of the 2-6-0 Mogul locomotive still resplendent in peacetime green, and went to the gate to collect tickets from the dozen or so alighting passengers. About half of these boarded a hybrid bus-van, boasting the legend 'George Hotel'. The rest sought waiting cars. A dozen passengers off, nobody on; an apparently endless cascade of empty boxes from the guard's van. The George Hotel vehicle backed away from the railings and turned up the hill to the town rather more than a mile off, followed by a couple of cars. The signalman closed the doors of two empty compartments, hung the single-line token over the railings near the bottom of the signalbox steps, and went to help porter and guard throw out more empty boxes and occasional parcels.

'Good thing when they put the special back on.'

'Dunno about that,' was the signalman's contribution. ' 'Tis a nuisance 'aving to be 'ere for 'e.'

Well after the arriving passengers were out of sight, the porter kicked a couple of boxes clear of the van's door, the guard waved his green flag, and this being the Great Western where custom forbade any movement without warning, the driver sounded a shrill whistle and the train progressed towards Barnstaple.

The signalman picked up the token, as he returned to his box, put it into its instrument and sounded the 2-pause-1 'train out of section' signal to the previous station, Bishop's Nympton and Molland. No acknowledgement, the signalman (woman, I was later to discover) not being at home. But the 2-bell 'train entering section' signal sent to the

These two early photographs, taken shortly after the opening of the impoverished Devon & Somerset Railway in 1873, show South Molton in the days of Brunel's broad gauge of 7 ft $0\frac{1}{4}$ in. Platforms were widened when the gauge was narrowed but buildings on both sides remained unchanged till the end. The main station buildings are in fact still there, used by light industry.

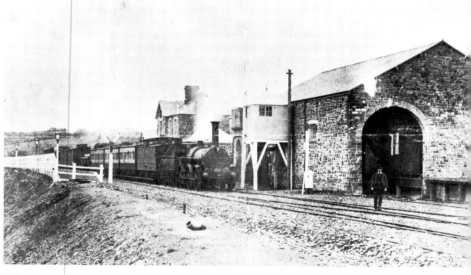

next station, Filleigh, was duly answered. After throwing three signals back to danger, the signalman then came down to help the porter sort the heap of boxes and miscellaneous goods left behind; they worked silently to a well-tried ritual. Long cylinders of Calor gas were neatly balanced on a barrow held upright; parcels, including Harris' sausages and Lyons' cakes, were placed on another barrow and wheeled into the parcels office. Empties were stacked in various heaps for later collection. These boxes I learnt were for rabbit traffic, the special mentioned in the conversation being a rabbit special – the only one in the country – that began at this station during the peak of the season.

This was my first meeting with a country train, the 10.17 on one of the first days in September 1942. Leaving a bomb-threatened area, the previous evening my family had arrived in the town up the hill, at first duly staying in the George; and this morning I had found a footpath across fields with a view of the station and its activities, arriving just in time for the train.

It was love – real passion – at first sight. You need to have experienced it to understand. It was not just the steam engine, compelling though that was with its bright fire consuming prime South Wales steamless coal, its boiler uttering a gentle groan unique to that type. Nor was it just the signalling, enthusiastically though I took to working the box when invited into it and gaining the trust of the signalman. It was no one thing, any more than a superb landscape painting is any one of its ingredients. It was the total railway in the countryside, serving it as part of it, the smell of steam and oil, the people arriving and departing, the ticket racks in the booking office from which you could tell how many people had gone where in the previous day and what the takings had totalled (£30 on a good day), the rule book I read by oil lamp with the tail of the signalman's dog gently flopping on the lino asking for attention. The trains brought special joy, especially when we crossed two passenger services or had a cattle special as well as the ordinary goods in the yard together. There were bicycles left in store one could ride when the station was deserted, parcels worth curious glances, the walk along the point-rodding on the first part of the route to a bridge over a river where one of the station-masters of my time spent much of his day fishing. If one was ever bored, the omnibus telephone always had potential.

South Molton signalbox (note the nestboxes and horseshoe) with signalman Frank Gill to whom in a sense this book is dedicated.

All stations on the branch shared a common telephone circuit, supplemented only by individual circuits between neighbouring boxes. Thus though a box-to-box message reporting the running of an additional freight might be passed down the line on the 'private' circuits, any call more than one station away had to be on the omnibus. Each station had its own answering code and the signalmen learnt to come to attention when their own rang, simply not hearing the others. 'Anyone on?' one would ask, picking up the earpiece and only pressing out the code of the required station on the button if the omnibus was vacant. To get Exeter headquarters, South Molton had to call Dulverton and be switched to a second circuit; it was Exeter from which extra cattle wagons for great market day would be ordered, or the ailing condition of a 'Dukedog' reported. And from Exeter came messages using the GW's own code: Crocodile was a type of long slung bogie wagon that everybody knew, Coral was less familiar, a wagon for glass in crates, Gadfly was a flat truck for aeroplane traffic. After taking down a message the signalman tried to work it out with minimum resort to the code book.

But most calls on that omnibus circuit were not on railway business: one found oneself eavesdropping on staff discussing their domestic troubles, handing out advice on kids or eelworm. As only the signalbox was on the system, the stationmaster had to come there and chat in front of the signalman. The only public telephone was in the parcels office, with an alarm bell in the signalbox since that was staffed far longer than the rest of the station. Working six days a week in alternate shifts from before 6 in the morning till nearly 11 at night, the signalman's basic 70s. was usually taken by overtime to over £5 a week.

South Molton then had five daily passenger trains each way between Taunton and Barnstaple. Except at peak times they had three coaches, two non-corridor and one corridor, the latter being included in the formation (so I was told years later) following an unfortunate incident caused by lack of a lavatory on a 45-mile trip to Barnstaple that took all but two hours. No Sunday trains ran in wartime, but a notice still pinned up in the signalbox announced the timings of a pre-war summer one, and before the war on summer weekdays a lunchtime restaurant-car had come down so far as South Molton, where it was shunted to an up train crossed in

In late June 1958, a summer Saturday Wolverhampton–Ilfracombe train proudly displaying express headlamps and destination boards pauses at a deserted platform.

the station. Even in the war one summer Saturday train ran through from Ilfracombe.

Two of the three daily goods each way stopped here, one with its station truck opposite the parcels office, one to shunt for a lengthy period (up to two hours) in the yard. The third ran as an express, the only train making use of the automatic token exchange apparatus, similar to that for exchanging mailbags at speed. The rabbit special ran for about half the year: only two bogie vans, but they absorbed an incredible quantity of rabbits, brought in by a procession of vintage vans and horse-drawn vehicles. It was in the station during two early-evening hours when otherwise things were dead and staff could wander off to catch rabbits themselves or to fish – providing they checked the special notice booklet, issued weekly. The signalman at the next station towards Barnstaple, Filleigh, once missed the printed announcement of a special, which had to be held at South Molton for an hour until he innocently returned. Occasional specials were needed since all regular goods trains which left Taunton made up 28 wagons, the maximum on that hilly road. Not infrequently a train ground to a standstill on a gradient, the engine taking half the wagons forward to the nearest station and returning for the rest. The GW did everything possible to route traffic for Barnstaple and beyond via Exeter and the Southern, as before the war staff had jealously kept business on their own system.

To improve its links with North Devon, especially Ilfracombe, in the 1930s the GW began improving the branch and installed the automatic token exchangers. After a shabby history – everything had been meanly done by the local company who built the line and who once owed £500,000 arrears of debenture interest – the branch could have been set to realize its potential. But then the GW and Southern, though still competing keenly for traffic, reached agreement to spend no more money on their respective lines to Barnstaple.

South Molton's main buildings, in stone, were on the down platform. Part of a house occupied by the goods clerk, the station consisted of a large general waiting-room with a small booking office leading off it (passengers bought their tickets in a corridor displaying the wartime notice 'Is your journey really necessary?'), the parcels office with large sliding doors to the platform, and a small ladies' room – with the one respectable lavatory. The signalbox was only a few steps away. On the up platform opposite was merely a small and badly-neglected open shelter: unlike most stations, South Molton was signalled so that up as well as down

Two glimpses of the engineering works that made the Devon & Somerset Railway so expensive. Mogul No. 7303 leaves the short tunnel near Venn Cross, and another 2-6-0 crosses the Tone Valley between Venn Cross and Wiveliscombe with an almost empty train in 1964.

trains could use the down platform, and the up (reached by ramp, there being no bridge) was only needed when two trains were being crossed. That was avoided if neighbouring stations could decently be persuaded to do the crossing there. The goods clerk and his assistant had a separate office next to the goods shed. The yard was a large one with about half a dozen sidings, including a curved line beside a row of warehouses, from which seeds and fertilizers were distributed around the area by a fleet of lorries coming and going in the yard. The warehouses stretched almost to the Tinto Inn, a real railway pub where passengers would wait if trains were late and cider was generously bought by the staff – including some for the men at Filleigh who had no pub.

Running the station establishment absorbed considerable time and money. Fires burned all the year round in the signalbox where there was no other means of cooking, and most of the year in the dank booking office. Paraffin for the heater in the parcels office came from the lamp hut; lamps in the dozen signals, including the two distant signals each a third of a mile away, had to be topped-up daily, which took the youngest member of staff much of his morning. Beside the nearby gangers' hut the diesel trolley used for most of the maintenance work between stations stood on its own short piece of track; it could be lifted on to similar pieces of track out in the country beside huts provided with intermediate block token apparatus. This contrivance often caused trouble and brought the signalling maintenance gang down from Dulverton. The locomotive water supply could also need attention.

Our passengers were not that numerous considering South Molton itself had a population of around 4,000 and the station served an area with over 15,000 people. Few people then needed to leave their own district, and Barnstaple was more easily reached by bus. The frequency with which Henry Williamson (of *Tarka* fame) had travelled from Filleigh to Bristol to broadcast was occasionally commented on; it was not unusual to find a young lad called into the forces was making his first train trip. On normal days perhaps 200 people came in and out, twice that number at the monthly great market or the twice-yearly sheep fair held in pens near the station. But nearly everyone making a journey of importance, joining up, coming home on leave, off to the funeral of a distant relative, used the train. The staff knew almost all their passengers; even strangers

114

would normally be met by a local person. The staff also watched the parcels traffic with interest. In freight terms it was a far more important station, with a monthly turnover of up to 600 or even 700 wagons.

For two years I spent most of my spare time at that station. Those winter evenings in the blacked-out, airless signalbox when the down train which brought the largest number of passengers was late, and steadily more people would invite themselves in, are particularly memorable. First the postman waiting for mailbags, then the driver of the George bus, drivers of taxis from various villages, retired railwaymen, friends and acquaintances of any of them with an excuse to introduce themselves and wait in warmth – though others would have chosen the Tinto. The only person absent might have been the signalman, issuing an odd ticket to Barnstaple or answering the public telephone; staff were scarce and nobody else on duty. So it would be left to a fifteen-year-old to accept the train from Bishop's Nympton and Molland and ten minutes later pull the levers. 'Be careful lad', one of the men would feel constrained to warn, as others sang 'She'll be coming round the mountain when she comes.' But while it might look complicated, six pairs of catch points contributing to the 33-lever frame, it was all far too interlocked to make error likely. Only when an engine was running round its train and two-thirds of the levers had to be used, some twice, did you have to think, though the catch points were perpetual traps for loose-coupled goods, and the driver who stopped to pick up a token by hand right over the catch points because his locomotive was not equipped with automatic exchanger gave us a breathless moment. We only pulled over the distant signal when exchanging was to be done automatically, at 40 miles an hour, and should have been told if an engine lacked an exchanger. Occasionally a token would miss and disappear down the embankment as the train squealed to a standstill.

There were again special occasions, such as the time that a goods train was derailed at one of the catch points, for no better reason than that its driver descended the hill out of control. For sheep fairs South Molton had its own special train of 'cattle' wagons, involving steam swearing since the siding leading to the cattle dock was short and to marshal the final train with trucks in the right order was endlessly difficult; and visiting buyers and others used the station, with its phone and its table for writing on, as headquarters. Not that all could write: several would ask for assistance, and one regular buyer who spent what seemed a fortune each fair tipped generously to have his letters confidentially whispered aloud to him. It was not unusual for local people to place a cross instead of a signature in the parcels book.

Then there was the time the lady from a local big house offended the porter by tipping him a penny (an *old* penny) for stowing her innumerable pieces of luggage in the van. Readily accepting the signalman's irreverent suggestion, as the train was leaving, he opened the door on the 'mean old bugger': 'Your paper, my lady,' he said, politely handing up a copy of the *Daily Herald*. Or the night when two truckloads of boisterous bullocks were unloaded at the platform because snow had made it difficult to work the points into the yard. The beasts disappeared into the night, frightened the wits out of customers emerging from the Tinto, and had to be rounded up with the help of others from the pub and a couple of passengers. General Eisenhower's special train passed through; the signal-woman at the next station rang up in tears to say she'd pulled the lever under a guard's van and derailed it and what, oh what, should she do; a policeman arrived to investigate complaints that rabbits were being swapped, small ones caught by the staff being left in the place of large ones that turned up in the local market; a ganger's wife who yesterday had lost the outward half of a ticket saw fit to use it today.

But the same trains performing the same tasks ran day by day, and though the signalman muttered that even nationalization might not prevent buses and lorries taking over when peace returned, it all had a solid feeling of permanence while much of the rest of the world was being torn to bits. The war was usually remote, though an occasional boy limped off a train battle-scarred, and the start of doodlebug raids on London brought fresh waves of evacuees. One summer's day several hundred on their way further down the branch had their first fill of country air: misunderstanding the whereabouts of the up evening train, I halted theirs to 'cross' it at our station instead of the next. As the pause became embarrassing, the burly, beaming guard came into his own and with the aplomb of an experienced tour courier ensured nobody wasted the hiatus, pointed out the rabbits, explained milking routines to the children, and delighted all by answering questions in an exaggerated Devon brogue.

Between Taunton and Barnstaple, only Dulverton was more important than
South Molton, not for its own traffic but as junction for the Exe Valley branch
to Tiverton and Exeter. A Taunton train arrives while the Exe Valley auto-
cars wait in the branch platform.

With the same backcloth of Somerset hills, an Exe Valley train approaches
Dulverton. Note the automatic token exchanger, used only for Taunton–
Barnstaple traffic.

The Taunton–Barnstaple line in fact became steadily busier for a time after the war, as Ilfracombe and other North Devon resorts benefited from universal holidays with pay, and farming also became more prosperous and fertilizer sales soared. Up to a dozen trains, some sporting destination boards and carrying hundreds rather than dozens of passengers, passed through each way on summer Saturdays. But inevitably they swore never to endure such a slow journey again. It was agony in a non-corridor compartment with twelve occupants, including several children. So people still using trains for their holiday began choosing places reached more expeditiously, and long-distance motor coaches made special inroads in North Devon before the private car became universal. More goods arrived in the manufacturer's or distributor's own lorry. Ultimately it was the privately-owned C-licence vehicle that killed most country stations. Coal's role in the rural economy declined with the massive electrification schemes of the post-war years. Myxomatosis ended the rabbit trade. All costs soared and the wage bill alone exceeded the branch line's total takings.

First – in the late 1950s – to go was not part of the railway service proper but the Tinto, hit by a declining number of passengers and better timekeeping which gave less opportunity for drinking. Then through goods to Barnstaple were routed via Exeter, leaving a single daily goods to Dulverton three days a week and on to South Molton only the other three. The summer Saturday through trains to Ilfracombe were also sent by Exeter. At the end (services ceased in October 1966) the single-coach diesel always had ample room, though life at places like East Anstey and Yeo Mill has never been the same since they lost a service buses were unable to replace. Perhaps a twentieth of the goods that used to arrive by train now make part of their journey to South Molton by the main line, but ironically many more local people use a train than ever before, because more take day trips to London, making their way to Taunton first.

The story could be repeated several thousand times up and down the length of the British Isles.

There was magic in the first glimpse through the trees of a down train passing the distant signal at speed. But many memories are of the men, some of whom remained regular correspondents until their death. The succession of unhappy stationmasters, apart from the first fishing enthusiast who continually boasted but never once, so far as I remember, had a fish to show, left the least impression. The signalman I knew best, and his tall colleague who arrived on a lady's bicycle of vast proportion – they chatted for about five minutes at the daily changeover, varied to suit their mutual convenience – both had their roots deep in country pursuits, and like most railwaymen were keen socialists. 'It's commonsense nationalization will save money. Take paint. It'll all be the same colour like the Post Office, there'll be one bloody great order at knockdown price.' The driver of the George bus had once run his own business, and though down on his luck vigorously defended capitalism.

One of my favourite drivers, for whom I would temporarily desert the signalbox, sadly felt the world was becoming unfit to live in. 'My wife and I decided we couldn't bring children into it. Those of us who are here have to make the best of it, but there's agony enough without more.' He was a favourite because he talked of engines and had a fund of old railway knowledge. Everyone of course reckoned to be a weather prophet, and it was the skies, the birds and the crops, rather than trains or the battles in North Africa, that were the stuff of the exchanges between train and station staff.

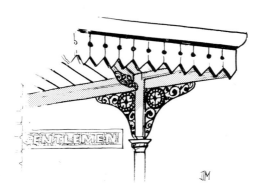

8 Deeper into the Countryside

It was perhaps inevitable that the country with the world's best country stations should be the most inflexible over providing cheap country transport. The problem is not new. For a century various organizations have been lobbying for more sensible arrangements. One such organization was the Light Railway Commissioners who for decades hammered away about the need for 'co-operation and co-ordination rather than ... competition, between light railway enterprise and road-motor transport'.

An earlier chapter touched upon the generally happy relationship, through the railway department of the Board of Trade, between the State and the free-enterprise railway companies. But the Board of Trade even more than the individual companies fell into the trap of regarding any railway as a railway, subject to the same rules and regulations. As safety and other requirements increased, so the cost of providing a line for the lightest traffic also went up – until it became prohibitive. To cite an example, it was compulsory to provide a raised platform so that passengers could walk straight into their compartment; so platforms were provided to serve tiny hamlets, and more expense might be incurred in shunting mixed trains to the passenger platform to pick up a solitary schoolboy, while in most of the rest of the world a movable platform with steps would be lowered, or a simple wooden pair of steps dropped beside the train on the ballast.

Branch lines were generally over-signalled. An army could have been carried in safety where only scores of people ever travelled. Because stations were so costly, they were often not provided at all where there might still have been useful traffic; and one could argue that in the motor age more lives would have been saved had the railways reduced safety standards – more people would then have gone by train, which would still have been safer than buses and cars. The simpler branch lines of

Continental countries were not dangerous, but they did serve the public, wandering cheaply between villages, not sticking to valley bottoms with the arrogance of main lines. And most countries did not demand such an expensive preliminary legal process as the full British Act of Parliament.

The need for greater flexibility had been seen as early as 1864 in the Railway Construction Facilities Act. That was supposed to make it possible for lines to be built without separate resort to Parliament – providing all landowners agreed. It also made the first mention of the light railway, built to a lower standard, the axle load to be limited to 8 tons and speed to 25 miles an hour. These powers achieved little, either because landowners would not sell and an Act of Parliament was still necessary or because the lines were built and equipped too ambitiously. People would not sacrifice traditional standards to expediency: a railway was a railway was a railway.

The Culm Valley Railway's prospectus boasted that 'everything being on a light scale commensurate with the traffic, the line can be made for £3,000 per mile, if the Landowners will part with the small quantity of land required, on favourable terms, and without putting the promoters to the expense of obtaining a special Act of Parliament.' But soon 'The Directors congratulate their co-Shareholders on having obtained an Act

An early roadside light railway, the Wantage Tramway.

of Parliament,' and 'It will be necessary to raise some additional capital'. The railway, so tortuous that after nationalization standard coaches could not be used, may have brought relief to its valley, but the shareholders thankfully sold to the Great Western for half the cost of construction: they had still built stations and other facilities too generously. Even the narrow-gauge Southwold Railway, delightfully suiting the character of the Suffolk seaside town, managed to saddle itself with a construction cost of £8,504 a mile though much of the material was allegedly salvaged from the unwanted Woosung Railway of China. Legislation and land expense were the chief trouble, though the Southwold did succeed in restoring prosperity to a place the main-line company refused to serve, and actually paid a dividend of 2 per cent for a few years. The little narrow-gauge Corris Railway in Wales, built at £1,814 a mile, and the standard-gauge Wisbech & Upwell, built over 8 miles of fens for £2,300 a mile, did make sense, filling gaps as should have been done on a much larger scale, and incidentally keeping themselves in business (for freight; passenger traffic naturally ceased earlier) until nationalization. The Wisbech & Upwell's coaches, one later to be featured in the film *The Titfield Thunderbolt*, had gangways with end steps, trains stopping anywhere on request.

After the agricultural depression at the end of the 1880s came more agitation for better transport for country people and goods, to make farming in remote areas more competitive. A Parliamentary committee went off to examine practice overseas, and in 1894 a Board of Trade conference led to the 1896 Light Railway Act, establishing the Light Railway

Culm Valley. Long after the loss of much of the capital by the original shareholders in the light railway, British Railways continued services, having to use a pair of gas-lit ex-Barry Railway coaches since standard stock would not take the sharp curves. Normally one of the pair sufficed. The fireman opens level-crossing gates for No. 1451 at Culmstock on the lunchtime train from Tiverton Junction in December 1971. And another locomotive of the same class, No. 1470, shunts its train back out of Hemyock's picturesquely-situated terminus, past the milk tanks which provided most of the latterday traffic. It was the creamery's unexpected closure in 1975 that led to the abandonment of the railway and the filling-in of the arch that had already been started to carry the M5.

122

Commissioners who could grant Light Railway Orders without Acts of Parliament. Land could be bought compulsorily, local authorities were for the first time encouraged to help provide country transport, and there could be treasury loans and grants. Applications poured in, 700 in the next quarter-century, but many were from local authorities seeking to extend town tramway systems, others from main-line railways hoping to reduce the cost of branch lines they were already committed to building as opposed to developing extra routes. Despite laudable intentions, the lines were still often built on main-railway principles, down the bottom of the valley, the station a mile or more from the village even if more shoddily constructed. Three-fifths of the 550 miles of light railways (excluding extensions of urban street tramways) built by the end of 1918 were owned or worked by existing main-line companies, and this included all the mileage (80) aided by free Treasury grants and part of that aided by loans. Only 23 miles of independent lines were financed partly by Treasury loans. Of the million pounds made available for loans, little more than £200,000 had been used.

The Light Railway Commissioners themselves were far from happy. In 1920 the Minister of Transport, Sir Eric Geddes, appointed a Light Railways (Investigation) Committee, which reported next year. Too late, it confirmed the benefits of Continental methods of financing and build-

Southwold's derelict terminus in the 1930s after the railway had done all it could for the local economy – though it would have helped to have a harbour branch before fishing had collapsed – and passenger traffic had been lost to buses then allowed to travel at 20 mph compared with the train's 16.

In contrast Upwell station on the Wisbech & Upwell (passenger train at left) was handling much of its district's business at the same time.

ing real rural light railways. Like the Commissioners it emphasized the need for an overall rail-road policy, aimed 'at a solution of the problem by way of co-operation and co-ordination rather than of competition, between light railway enterprise and road-motor transport respectively.' This and most of the other sound advice was of course ignored.

Britain indeed wasted every opportunity to develop basic, integrated country transport services at economic prices. The railways, notably the Great Western, were themselves bus pioneers from 1904 onward, and developed substantial road networks. Yet, in the heady competitive years of the mid-1920s, some of these routes were along the roads used by independent operators and companies in the two growing bus groups, British Electric Traction and Tilling. At one stage it looked as though the railways would aggressively defend their routes and develop more, but in the event a wretched 'controlled monopoly' was decided upon. The railways invested equally in the BET and Tilling companies. Large sums of railway capital thus helped the development of bus services while the railways dropped. The Road Traffic Act of 1930 then effectively protected the monopoly of stage-service buses already in operation, leaving only trains to compete with them.

The railway companies, BET and Tillings set up joint railway-bus committees to prevent the worst excesses of competition (often successfully) and to provide more positive co-ordination (usually unsuccessful). Rarely was thought given to exploiting the advantages of both train and bus for different parts of a through journey, and with only a few exceptions (mainly in the Southern Railway's West Country territory) bus-connection times were not stated in the timetables, no through tickets being available. The joint committees found it easier to prick initiative than to provoke it: for instance, as the Western National Omnibus Company complained that a proposed train excursion fare for a special event in Minehead was too cheap, the train never ran. Railwaymen more often enjoyed the social contact of being directors of the local bus company than taking up the challenge the appointment gave.

Inevitably, buses running from village centres to market squares at cheaper fares would cream off the best local traffic, leaving the railways to provide connections for long-distance passengers and to carry specific categories of people, such as mothers with prams – perambulators in railway parlance – and schoolchildren; the railways always had cheaper season-ticket rates. After nationalization, 'co-operation' was even fainter-hearted, and now the railways' timetables have dropped even the few bus-connection times once quoted – though the information is even more needed, many important towns of over 10,000 people being left without trains.

From the investor's point of view it may be as well that all those light railway schemes proposed under the 1896 Act did not come to fruition, much though they would have added to the railway scene for enthusiasts. Many of those built were indeed dearly loved by their local communities – the Welshpool & Llanfair, for instance, one of a number in central Wales. Typically, there had been much talk about building a 9-mile line from the busy little market town of Llanfair Caereinion, to the main railway at Welshpool, for years before the Light Railway Act was passed. The Act spurred new attempts, and a Light Railway Order was obtained in 1899. It laid down that the line, of 2 feet 6 inch gauge, had to be operated by an existing company, so it was leased to the Cambrian (which kept 60 per cent of gross receipts) for 99 years. The cost of the 9 miles winding through mountainous country – in the Pass of Golfa half a mile was at the very steep gradient of 1 in 29 – was £47,900, nearly twice the estimate. Local councils as well as the Treasury contributed.

'*Beg pardon, driver, but there's an axle box overheating under my compartment.*'

Opened in 1903, the railway immediately benefited its community. But it was not profitable. There was no major industry or staple traffic here, and weekly cattle specials did not sufficiently supplement takings from coal and general merchandise, passengers and mail. So only *The Earl* and *Countess* were built instead of the three engines planned, and normally only one was steamed. Signals came down in 1911; hardly surprising since two years later the total receipts were £3,049. But minor improvements were still made; the railway was serving its community well, *Llanfair Jinny* as it was nicknamed usually running mixed and carrying com-

Temporarily without her nameplate, the Countess *simmers away right beside Welshpool Market to which she has brought a load of cattle, waiting to return with another; 1951.*

mercial travellers and the goods they took orders for, schoolchildren and most local comers and goers: there were seven intermediate stopping places. If the police wanted to know of anybody's movements, the guard was the first person to help.

In 1923 the line passed to the Great Western, who put on its own buses in competition with the trains – as a preliminary to killing them, it was said. Passenger traffic ceased in 1931. But general merchandise and those weekly cattle specials continued until 1956 (we forget how recently the motor lorry finally conquered all) – and that was late enough for enthusiasts to get together and rescue the line as an attraction in its own right. The side-tank 0-6-0 *The Earl* and *Countess* now appear in many holiday-makers' films, and the Welshpool & Llanfair has an honourable place among the 'great little trains of Wales'. Among these, the historic Ffestiniog Railway, open in 1836 for slate traffic, is currently building a major narrow-gauge tunnel to restore access to Blaenau Ffestiniog flooded by a reservoir; its Tanybwlch station, set in a horseshoe curve among ancient oaks, is surely the epitome of country station excellence. The Talyllyn was also built for slate traffic, and was the first line to be rescued by volunteers; and the Vale of Rheidol, British Rail's only narrow-gauge and steam-operated line, built under the 1895 Act, was a commercial flop but dearly loved.

Down in Devon the Lynton & Barnstaple, built to the same British standard narrow gauge, 1 foot $11\frac{1}{2}$ inches, as the Ffestiniog and the Vale of Rheidol, was closed less than forty years after its opening, before running trains for pleasure and preservation was fashionable. With its genteel engineering works (Chelfham viaduct still stands), its neat villa-like stations, and a winding route on the foothills of Exmoor that fitted perfectly into the countryside it served, this was one of the most beautiful of lines.

Though open in May 1898, it had an Act of Parliament and was not a true Light Railway. Lynton was further away from a railway than any place of comparable population in England, and with backing from the tourist trade the authorized capital of £70,000 was healthily over-subscribed. But then we have the usual tale of woe, costs exceeding expectation (£5,000 per mile instead of the estimated £2,500), a bankrupt contractor, and a final capital liability that made even the $\frac{1}{2}$ per cent dividend paid on ordinary shares from 1913 to 1921 look miraculous. Though there was a healthy flurry of activity on Fridays, Barnstaple market day, the evening train leaving with two engines (one worked back with several empty coaches from an intermediate station), to the terminus station, 700 ft above sea level and 250 ft above Lynton itself, tourist traffic did not grow as hoped. Among the promoters was Sir George Newnes, who made two attempts to carry Ilfracombe people to the railway at Blackmore; the second used what was in fact the first bus feeder-service for a railway, but local magistrates prosecuted when a vehicle was found going a little faster than 8 miles per hour, and the buses were sold to the GW for use on the Helston–Lizard service, normally said to have been the first railway-operated bus. Indeed, the Lynton & Barnstaple had not actually owned its feeder.

The Southern Railway became owner in 1923 and made some improvements, but more important for the area generally was the regrading of two steep sections of the Barnstaple–Lynton road. It was by this road that representatives of the twin towns of Lynton and Lynmouth travelled to put their case for the retention of the railway. The Southern adamantly closed it at the end of the 1935 season, with a double-headed train of nine coaches echoing its way over the Exmoor foothills – despite a last-minute hope that it could be saved by the 'in perpetuity' reference in its Act of Parliament.

Only ten years before the Lynton & Barnstaple closed, one of the last light railways of major length opened a few miles away, the grandly-named North Devon & Cornwall Junction Light Railway, from Torrington across the no-man's-land of the North Devon plateau country to Petrockstowe, Hatherleigh and Halwill Junction. Hatherleigh still best remembers the railway, built partly with local money, for the riots and murder during its construction; the station was 2 miles from the town, the route a snail's pace 20 miles, instead of 7 by road, to Okehampton, the place most people visited. The first part, as far as Petrockstowe, replaced a narrow-gauge tramway of the North Devon Clay Company, and clay traffic continued (and still continues) on the standard-gauge light railway, winding alongside brooks and making every deviation to save earthworks. But for many years it was positively unusual for a single passenger to be carried by either of the two daily trains south of Petrockstowe.

130

'We had two people on Monday, Mr & Mrs X going to see their daughter in Bude,' I remember the guard telling me by way of justifying his existence. Finding various excuses to visit this living but empty museum over the years, I once drove the evening train from Halwill and arrived at Petrockstowe so early (partly because the timetable allowed for unwanted shunting at Hole and Hatherleigh) that the crew played cards for half an hour in the station and still reached Torrington ahead of schedule.

For two or three decades, a single empty coach (empty apart from a few pieces of luggage, and at busy times rabbit boxes piled in the first compartment as well as the guard's van) passed through Hatherleigh each way twice daily, the driver, fireman, guard and signalman being amazed if a passenger was seen. It was as if Waterloo had forgotten the line, or it was deemed indecent to close a railway opened as recently as 1925. These were not of course the only empty trains in Britain; even before the war there was a sporting chance of travelling from Harpenden to Hemel Hempstead, or from the Mound to Dornoch, in splendid isolation. But nowhere else, before, during and after the war, under private enterprise and nationalization, could you so certainly count on having the show

Barely one passenger a week used Hatherleigh's well-kept station still served by two one-coach trains each way daily, almost invariably empty, though this was 1959, more than a decade after nationalization and a time of mounting railway losses.

to yourself for the whole 20 miles, the show including the timetable printed in *Bradshaw*, which even gave the early-closing days of the two or three shops in villages along the route, and including holding up cars and buses that actually had people in them at the numerous unprotected level crossings. The most serious of many level-crossing accidents was between a full excursion bus and an empty train.

The North Devon & Cornwall Junction Light Railway should surely have belonged to Britain's only group of independently-owned lines, Associated Railways, the 'Colonel Stephens lines' – built or maintained to rudimentary standards, serving areas of sparse population or crossing the country in directions people did not generally go. In fact this railway was engineered by the Colonel, always ready for a commission, but it was not one of the seven lines he managed on a day-to-day albeit somewhat remote basis from his office in Tonbridge.

Philip Shaw Stephens (1868–1931) is the enigmatic figure of the country railway. Little is known about his personal life except that he was single (not surprising in view of his passion for his far-flung railways), living mainly in hotels and clubs. Tall, with clipped moustache, bowler hat and cane, he had a distinct military bearing, and though he could be kind he was not always loved. Apart from military service, his whole life was devoted to this curious string of semi-derelict lines; the more rural the surroundings the greater the challenge. When aged only 22 he was resident engineer of the Paddock Wood & Cranbrook Railway, and in 1895 he proudly equipped as well as built the Rye & Camber Tramway – for which he designed an Akroyd-Stewart compression-ignited diesel tractor, though the directors played safe and stuck to steam. Next came the Hundred of Manhood & Selsey Tramway, its $7\frac{1}{2}$ miles built for a modest £19,000.

After the 1896 Light Railway Act the Colonel rushed around advising on new schemes, providing engineering and management services, and investing his own money. The seven lines he managed himself included the East Kent, West Sussex Light, Weston, Clevedon & Portishead, and Shropshire & Montgomeryshire Light, all truly lines of character on which no new piece of equipment was ever purchased if anything second-hand would do. Even his famous back-to-back petrol-engine railbuses had nothing more elaborate than a secondhand Wolseley Siddeley car

132

Col. Stephens.

chassis as starting point. Sheer devotion succeeded where formal management was lacking, and if the traffic did not provide enough for the week's
wages he dipped into his own pocket.

The Colonel would arrive unexpectedly, order a special train and make
an inspection, cigars being handed out to staff if all was well, blistering
memos following if not. At least the trains kept going, and delightful
period pieces some of them were, even by the First World War. It was
his growing reputation that led to the Colonel's least happy appointment,
as chief engineer and locomotive superintendent of the Ffestiniog Railway, suffering severely from a cutback in slate traffic, and its ill-conceived
sister the Welsh Highland, perhaps the ultimate in railways linking places
with little demand for transport via country with none at all. The
Ffestiniog, with its ancient works at Boston Lodge, had been a proud

133

Three outposts of the Stephens Empire: a railcar with trailer rolls over the pointwork of the Weston, Clevedon & Portishead Light Railway; Gazelle with branch train at Kinnerley Junction on the Shropshire & Montgomery; and a Ford railcar at Tenterden, headquarters of the Kent & East Sussex, in 1931, the year before it went into receivership.

self-contained little world drawing on local talent, indelibly Welsh, which an itinerant English expert of military disposition arriving as chief executive could never penetrate. Orders were forgotten, overlooked, grudgingly started and again forgotten, the staff sometimes mutinous. Such scant money as could be afforded for improvements was usually wasted, and maintenance standards dropped till trains began breaking down almost daily, staff merely hoping it would happen near enough to a road for easy rescue of passengers by charabanc.

Read the history of the Ffestiniog of the 1920s and 1930s and it is indeed surprising that the double-boilered Fairlie locomotives were still around by the outbreak of war, leave alone to be rebuilt in the postwar revival. The Ffestiniog lingered just long enough to be resuscitated. Not one of the seven lines that were the core of Col. Stephens' business is now with us, but many remember the grassgrown tracks and the quaint assortments of rolling stock, sometimes switched between railways, the posters urging villagers to 'support the local line' and the advice to 'travel across country away from the dusty and crowded roads on home-made steel instead of imported rubber'. A delightful range of hardware is already collected for a Stephens museum at Tenterden.

There should have been other Col. Stephenses running other groups of utility-built and cheaply-run country railways; almost however badly maintained they would have been safer for local traffic than the parallel road. Col. Stephens was but one of many critics of waste on ordinary country railways; what would he have thought had he ridden on the last special train over the Yealmpton branch in Devon? The diesel multiple unit maintained a smooth 45 mph over a track which for the past two decades had carried only three short freights a week. That speed should have been impossible: the tracks should have been disappearing into nature, 15 or 20 miles an hour the maximum through the sheer discomfort of anything faster.

But a railway was a railway, and the public mocked the Col. Stephens lines and anything run cheaply enough to make economic sense. Take the Kelvedon & Tollesbury Light Railway. True, its junction with the main line was scarcely 40 miles from Liverpool Street, and the contrast between London's busiest terminus and a slow mixed train wandering over the Essex marshes a mere hour and a half later was as keen as

But the Kent & East Sussex miraculously survived to be nationalized when its service was greatly improved. The afternoon Rolvenden to Headcorn train is here approaching Tenterden in 1953.

anything experienced by air travellers even in the jet age. But why should passengers have been surprised that there were no signals because 'the solitary engine, fantastic as are some of its tricks, has apparently not acquired the art of running into itself'? Or be amazed when the fireman climbed down to open the gates at a crossing over a main road? Or laugh at the old, worn-out carriage bodies providing shelters on the slabs of tarmac serving as platforms?

The Kelvedon & Tollesbury served its district well, carrying up to 1,000 people a day, and a sizeable part of the nation's jam supply from Wilkinson's Tiptree factory despatched to literally thousands of different stations. It was one of the more successful light railways built under the 1896 Act (the Treasury contributed about £16,000 or just over one-third of the estimated cost), and if there is any criticism with hindsight it must be that its Light Railway Order insisted (like many others) on its being

operated by the neighbouring main-line company instead of leaving it free to run itself maybe even more cheaply. Of course its trains were quaint, the shunting of strings of jam-laden wagons – the factory had its own railway system – while passengers had to wait; quite different from main-line practice. But even today that corner of Essex does not live at London's pace. It is a monument to British obstinacy that railways were not allowed to develop even more of a local character, according to the country they served and the traffic they carried – that more passengers were not asked to show their tickets to a guard climbing from compartment to compartment while the train was rattling along, instead of having time-wasting formal examinations at the last stop before termini and junctions without a full-time ticket collector. A pity too that when a line like this performed as it should, it could in no way seek protection from competition in the form of a bus operated by someone keener on being his own boss than on helping the transport scene.

9 Ireland and the Isle of Man

If Britain built its country railways over-generously, those of Ireland were extravagantly prodigal. For a start the standard gauge for this sparsely-populated and mainly impoverished land was a luxurious 5 feet 3 inches, more costly in engineering works and maintenance than the 4 feet $8\frac{1}{2}$ inches of Britain and most of Europe and North America. Unlike Britain, Ireland had a standard narrow gauge but, at 3 feet, even that was only 6 inches less than the main lines of countries like Japan, New Zealand and South and East Africa. Again engineering works were often unnecessarily expensive for the traffic. Gauges of 4 feet $8\frac{1}{2}$ inches and something between 2 feet and 2 feet 6 inches but with transporter wagons for standard-gauge vehicles would have saved millions and improved traffic.

Railway promoters saw fortunes round the corner; there was indeed no other route to such riches as the railway prospectuses offered. And as in Britain, only more so, the promoters allowed their financial judgement to be warped by local politics and jealousies. Duplicate routes were proposed. Each company had to have its station showpieces. Dublin had six major terminal points and even Londonderry four, including two narrow-gauge stations. Co-operation between neighbours was often minimal. Most narrow-gauge systems were isolated from each other, serving the poorer pockets of country not invaded by the 5 foot 3 inch lines, but County Donegal was almost entirely a narrow-gauge land, with two extensive systems, the County Donegal Railways and the Londonderry & Lough Swilly Railway, with a combined route mileage of 224. They met at Letterkenny but ungraciously ignored each other for the most part – and of course had separate Letterkenny stations, within shouting distance of each other. Only the occasional through excursion was allowed as an act of indulgence.

For the professional railway observer, anxious to see costs minimized and traffic maximized, Ireland was a frightening spectacle. I recall a visit to Stranorlar, headquarters of the County Donegal, where the former narrow-gauge corridor train of the Ballymena & Larne line was stabled under the extensive canopy of the bay platform. How often was it used, I asked. 'Too often,' was the reply: its usual passengers were Orangemen – 'Pity we have to carry them.' But, I suggested, they provided revenue. 'Revenue we'd be better without.' A crushing reply in the 1950s.

Not that Ireland totally lacked good trains. The weekly Cunard special for Dublin's North Wall to Queenstown (Cobh) was a luxurious link in the transatlantic service. Mail between London and Irish provincial centres travelled with amazing speed and regularity. English visitors to

Map of the narrow-gauge systems of County Donegal.

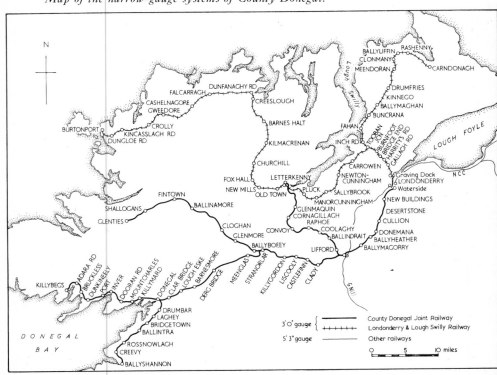

Stranorlar, headquarters of the County Donegal; note the clock tower which stood commandingly over the gentlemen's lavatory. 2-6-4 No. 6 Columbkille *prepares a special train.*

Killarney were cosseted. Even the well-to-do living in the larger cities had good business and seaside services with outstandingly spacious first-class carriages. But across country the picture was dismal: infrequent all-station trains rarely averaging much more than 25 mph, often less, with interminably long waits at junctions. Many trains were mixed; poor time-keeping was legendary; according to *Punch*, when the local dignitary complained he had missed the train because for the first time ever it seemed to have left on time, the stationmaster soothingly replied that wasn't it yesterday's train that had just gone.

Few country Irishmen ever moved beyond walking or riding distance in their own land, and though the village station might seem the centre of the universe for the monthly cattle fair, when two engines could be shunting in the yard, with business of all kinds being transacted in the waiting-room, and the gentlemen's continually under pressure, ordinarily

141

even the one or two stopping trains were a costly luxury. Travelling first class might be a solitary and prosperous priest, breviary-reading in splendid isolation. In the rest of the train, if it was Dublin or Cork bound from the country, there would be people the railway would only carry once: emigrants and soldiers serving the Empire on their way out of Ireland, not so much taking a last look at the scenery as frantically recounting old memories.[1]

Here is one description of emigrants leaving their local community. The station is Limerick Junction, one of the nation's major railway crossroads but set deep in the countryside, its curious layout requiring most trains to back into their platform.

We met with an incident highly illustrative of the ungovernable strength of the Irish temperament. A few emigrants to America were going to Cork via our train, and a host of their poor friends had assembled on the platform to bid them their last farewell. What a scene there was among these poor people to be sure! Such a handshaking, such kissing, such moaning and crying of 'The darlin'! Oh, the darlin'!' repeated again and again that although my sympathies are not easily moved by scenes of this kind I felt the tears coming to my eyes as I looked on this parting of friends and families, a parting which seemed to be the tearing to pieces of their very natures. As the train moved purposely slowly out of the station, the handshaking was renewed with greater vigour and the cry of 'The darlin', Oh, the darlin'!' became more frequent and violent, and it was only with great difficulty the guard could prevent the little crowd, which thronged the carriage window as the train moved, from getting dragged down between the train and the platform.

It is hard to grasp the scale of Irish emigration. Roughly speaking, the population halved, from eight million to four, between the completion of the first main lines and the time the railways lost their monopoly with the spread of cars and buses eighty years later. The station long closed is still remembered as the point where families split up; also as the channel for relief schemes for the starving. As in England, it was the gateway to the world, but here a grim and portentous gateway – quite often,

1. When it became necessary for would-be emigrants to visit the US Embassy in Dublin to obtain a visa, return tickets were issued at single fare 'on surrender of signed voucher from the Emigration Agent.'

*Alongside the public road, a view of the double-decker train on the Dublin &
Blessington after a single-decked but more frequent bus had taken most of the
traffic in the 1930s.*

built with cheap materials, no cosiness, poor furnishings, rarely any
flowers.

Irish railways worked with every conceivable disadvantage apart perhaps from cheap labour. Yet the system became extensive, totalling 3,442
miles at its peak in the 1920s. Agriculture became largely rail-orientated,
the monthly cattle fair governing the fortunes of the district providing,
among other things, the cash to buy the all-important fertilizers carried
around the country in surprising quantities. But by the 1870s it was clear
private enterprise could not fill in the rural network; and so legislation
and finance from government and local authority moved in.

The story is as complex as it is pathetic. Though there had been three
earlier Acts concerned with tramways running along public roads – as
quite a few rural and semi-rural routes did – the first major legislation
was the Tramways & Public Expenses (Ireland) Act of 1883, of course
passed in Westminster. Tramways promoters were empowered to ask the
Grand Jury of a county to arrange that baronies (district councils) through
whose territory the lines would pass should guarantee dividends up to
5 per cent on the working capital, and should also take over the 'complet-

ing, working and maintaining of the undertaking' should it fail in commercial hands. If the Grand Jury agreed, the Lord Lieutenant was to authorize the project, usually by an Order in Council, and keep an eye on its building and general position. Since few lieutenants bothered, or knew anything about railway construction anyway, and since the baronies whose funds were taxed had no direct powers of control, the lines were built wastefully, on too grand a scale for the traffic potentials; they represented bad value for money. They duly appeared as a drain on the rates, and the combination of bad service and higher rates was scarcely calculated to encourage the population to take to regular travel.

Take the Schull & Skibbereen in the far south-west, a district especially hit by famine and decline, as an example. Here was a narrow-gauge line only 15½ miles long, running beside the road most of the way (and therefore not incurring much by way of land costs), its capital totalling £57,000 with 5 per cent dividends guaranteed in perpetuity by the council. It never paid, its organization symbolized by departing trains from Skibbereen setting off backwards down a siding before they could head for Schull. It never could pay, with that cost of construction and a traffic that war-

The Schull & Skibbereen's No. 4 heading a typical train in 1937.

ranted only two daily trains except on fair days: there were no connections at Skibbereen for the main line, the concern being regarded as purely local, at least for passengers. Since its speed limit was anyway 15 mph, it could have been built far more economically to a narrower gauge, but 3 feet had become the legal Irish secondary gauge – though it was first adopted merely because several lines in the Ballymena district used it.

Before its official opening in 1886, a special to a pig fair at the main intermediate station, Ballydehob, had earned farmers better prices than normal; but such promise was blighted. Several times the service was totally withdrawn through failure of the locomotives (built for super-heating but, since the Board of Trade's inspecting officer said it was unnecessary for them to consume their own steam, the superheaters were removed), derailments caused by faulty track, and breakdown of the turntables. Things became so chaotic that, untypically, on repre-sentations from the ratepayers the Lord Lieutenant did stir himself and requested a Board of Trade enquiry. Back came the inspecting officer – his kind must have been valued patrons of the country's hotels – to hear an extraordinary tale of woe, and issue a report almost comically damning. That of course led to spending more money, including buying a fourth locomotive. And though the passengers never exceeded about 750 in one day, yet another machine was needed to keep things going in the 1910s.

This quotation from a booklet on the line perhaps demonstrates better than any generalization where the local *energy* went: not in making the railway efficient.

When the new engine arrived at Skibbereen, the matter of a name arose. At that time the 'All for Ireland League' (O'Brien's party) held the majority of seats on the local County Council and was at loggerheads with the Redmond-ites, whom most of the townsfolk and the Tramway staff supported. It was therefore decided that the engine be named *Conciliation*, after the party slogan ... However within a fairly short time, the Redmondites had secured the majority of political representation and, the Tramway staff having objected to the name, this was removed, the intention being to substitute *Hibernia* .. but when Sinn Fein became very active after the 1914–18 war, it was decreed that the locomotive be designated *Kent*, after Thomas Kent, executed in Cork Bar-racks after the 1916 rising.

It was soon clear the 1883 Act was not bringing forth enough new lines, and the deliberations of a Royal Commission on Irish Public Works appointed in 1886 led to the Light Railways (Ireland) Act of 1889. That enabled the Lord Lieutenant to make an Order in Council for a railway needed to develop a district, with Treasury support. The line had to be built by an existing company, no doubt to prevent another Schull & Skibbereen, but also ending the possibility of grassroots concerns serving their own district with the minimum of overheads. Well over a million pounds of public funds were consumed building nearly 250 miles of line under this and two minor Acts of 1890. Most were of standard gauge, many were branches that the large companies had intended building anyway.

Substantial areas of the rural west remained without public transport, and writers and politicians increasingly commented on the lack of real action. The final effort was the Light Railways (Ireland) Act of 1896, aiming to relieve pressure in the 'congested districts'. These were areas which had already lost substantial population but where landholdings were too small to support families and resources generally were overstretched. Building railways to create jobs was now part of the policy. Donegal benefited in particular, the narrow-gauge systems[1] extending in varying directions including an incredibly isolated 24 miles from Stranorlar to Glenties, a place of 1,000 people.

As in Britain, though everyone realized that attitudes were too rigid, this last Act was not going to change them. While they were built at all, railways were built as railways, with all the expensive appendages – Glenties station was a mini-village – and rules and regulations that would have prevented profits even if Ireland had grown prosperous in peace and railways had retained their monopoly; that was exactly what did not happen.

As early as the Fenian Rising of 1867, the Irish had learnt to disrupt their railways; then 1,000 men blocked the main Great Southern route from Dublin to Cork out in the country at Rathduff. The strains of the 1914–18 war were felt by Irish as by British railways and the Government took control. Then came the 1916 rising and the civil war or Troubles in the years either side of the creation of the Irish Free State in 1921. The County Donegal (now run by a joint committee representing the

1. Certain standard-gauge sections were narrowed as that system extended, to give the county a unified gauge.

146

owners, the Midland of England and the Great North of Ireland), the Londonderry & Lough Swilly, and the much more important Great Northern itself were among the railways finding themselves part in one country, part in another, and especially liable to damage and disruption. Not a train on the County Donegal, for instance, was immune from the risk of attack by armed gangs or derailment into river or field. The remoter the spot, the greater the risk. Signalmen daily expected their box to be burnt down. If troops were brought in, the staff might refuse to run the train.

The general manager, Henry Forbes, himself a political target, was an armed passenger when he saw his train crew held at gunpoint on the Ballyshannon branch. He slipped unseen out of his coach, along the ballast and on to the engine where shots were exchanged, chased the raiders across a cornfield, and caught one who slipped. The journey to Donegal

Among the railways straddling the new border and thus retaining its independence was the grandly-named but actually modest Sligo, Leitrim & Northern Counties, whose Manorhamilton headquarters are shown here. For its last 30 or so years the line kept going mainly on the cattle trade, millions of Sunday joints for Scotland and Northern England tables using it en route to Londonderry, Larne and Belfast. Closure in 1958 was forced through the Great Northern's withdrawal from Enniskillen.

then continued, the captive covered with his revolver. There being no policeman in Donegal – one wonders why! – they continued on the Londonderry train to Stranorlar.

And so it was in much of Ireland. The main line between Dublin and Cork was cut by the blowing up of Mallow Viaduct and for months the little station of Mourne Abbey was the busy terminus for Cork trains, buses providing a link to Mallow. The Dublin & South Eastern Railway received particularly rough treatment; a group of Irish railwaymen meeting today are still likely to talk nostalgically about spectacular wrecks and fires on that line: playing trains and wargaming on the grand scale. For the most part it was a very rural war, of course destroying many of Ireland's country houses, some of whose gaunt ruins may still be seen from the train on lines that survive.

Not much more than a third of the island's peak route mileage is now in use, but the rest only went after a long-drawn-out struggle. All companies wholly within the Free State were merged into the Great Southern in 1925. That prolonged the lives of many ailing rural and narrow-gauge concerns. Though little modernization was undertaken of the main lines before nationalization under Coras Iompair Eireann in 1950, at least the Great Southern could patch and mend, using its Inchicore Works at Dublin for rebuilding narrow-gauge stock, moving engines and plant from line to line as required.

The Cavan & Leitrim, the last narrow-gauge steam-operated line – it survived until 1959 through the accident of serving Ireland's only coal mine at Arigna – became a veritable working museum, its engines and coaches brought from various systems as they closed. In earlier days the Cavan & Leitrim had been another highly colourful, very political affair with frequent policy tugs of war, plenty of shootings in the Troubles, and the staff able to force the management to reinstate dismissed colleagues. Such was the power of the staff that when lorries first found their way into the railway's territory in 1926, 'Motor Lorry Committees' were formed at the principal stations and passed a resolution warning: 'Any railway employee or members of his household having further dealings with traders in the town who still persist in dealing with the motor lorries will be dealt with as follows: (i) we will ask the Railway Company to dispense with his service; (ii) we will prevent our organization giving him

148

any protection; (iii) members of the present organizations will refuse to work with him.'

Only one narrow-gauge system was really modernized in Eire: the erstwhile West Clare was given a new lease of life with CIE diesel cars and diesel locomotives for freight. For some years the diesels served this remote area well, but in its independent and steam days the West Clare epitomized the worst in expensively built, subsidized, unreliable Irish country railways. 'Perhaps it comes in two hours, perhaps it breaks down on the way,' ran a comic song by the genius of music hall, Percy French, who was summoned by the railway company for damages caused by his ridicule. He arrived late at the court hearing; his train had broken down. 'Do you think that ye can get the fire to light? Oh an hour you'll require, for the turf it might be drier.'

The history of Irish railways is full of unsuccessful attempts to burn turf in the locomotives instead of expensively imported coal. Though Ireland remained neutral during the 1939–45 war, little coal was available. Many branch lines closed for three years, and at times main-line services were down to a single train a week. Limerick Junction would resoundingly come to life after days of silence, as everyone who had to travel converged there and the engines of the two main-line trains which had been backed into their platforms faced each other a few yards apart. Nobody knew how long their journeys to Dublin and Cork would take. There were tales of journeys involving more than a dozen breakdowns, of the surrounding countryside being combed for combustible material to get the fire going again. If anything the position was even worse in the 1947 British fuel crisis. That led to early dieselization, though many routes provided with new diesels succumbed to road competition in the following years. Today there is no country branch line in Ireland; the last, to Loughrea, closing in 1975. Yet Ireland remains rail-conscious, its main-line services (most of a distinctly rural nature of course) being steadily upgraded.

Ulster has a different story. The Northern Counties Committee of the LMSR maintained a good system; bread for instance was distributed daily by passenger train to villages as well as towns. But when the Ulster Transport Authority took over (its acquisitions including the Belfast & County Down, almost bankrupted by the compensation exacted for a 1945 accident) in 1948, it had a distinctly anti-rail policy, and soon only the Dublin–Belfast–Londonderry links plus two local Belfast routes were left. Goods traffic was not steadily sorted out but killed outright. It did not improve the quality of Ulster life.

Of the systems straddling the border, two stand out, both already mentioned. The County Donegal Railways could have been an early casualty, but fought efficiently as well as bravely and provided something like a model service for a mountainous tract of empty country. It had a real leader in Henry Forbes, and shows how much can be achieved by a single man of calibre and authority – something seldom found in the troubled history of Irish concerns; most such people would have sought promotion elsewhere. Forbes lived and breathed the Donegal, and made it the best in narrow-gauge travel. He is especially remembered for his pioneering with diesel cars, those of 1931 being the first in the British Isles, though petrol cars had been in use for many years. (One can imagine Forbes's reaction when in 1926 a Free State customs official claimed that one was a bus and insisted on charging a $33\frac{1}{2}$ per cent duty.) As Edward M. Patterson, the historian of the Donegal, has commented, the important thing was that 'the bustling railcars, able to accelerate rapidly from the multitudinous stops, were treated as road buses would have been ... the crew's job was no sinecure; a constant watch had to be kept for passengers standing by the lineside, or huddled against a hedge out of the winter storms, the folding door had to be pulled open for them, and their ticket had to be issued if they had joined at an intermediate stop. Parcels had to be collected or set down, and "as an obligement" many a bottle of medicine was handed out through a railcar window or an urgent message called to the nearest neighbour down the line.'

The stud of bright-red tank locomotives, including a class of large superheated 2-6-4s, was of course maintained both for freight – the railway carried everything in the county – and special passenger duties including the Orangemen's excursions already mentioned: Forbes would

A page of diesel cars on the County Donegal. Top, as you would expect the barrels contain Guinness at this typical wayside station on the Ballyshannon branch. The middle picture shows trains – all trailing goods wagons – for Strabane, Ballyshannon and Killybegs at Donegal itself. Bottom, there were no passengers to enjoy the view of the Donegal hills in this railcar at Lough Eske in 1956.

150

151

not have shared the sentiment of the official quoted. Here was a railway which of course had to close as roads were improved and more flexible cars and lorries appeared, but which served its public well in its day and prolonged its life beyond that of its equivalents elsewhere. It went down in fine style on 31 December 1959 having put on its usual Christmas extras.

In contrast, the Great Northern (Ireland) was not just a rural concern but a major mixed railway, linking three important cities, with heavy suburban traffic in two of them, long-distance holiday expresses, and a host of cross-country and branch lines. It was Ireland's most efficient railway, and perhaps deservedly the last to retain the word Great in its title in the British Isles. Its blue engines, especially the 4-4-0s used on most expresses, were by far the smartest to be seen anywhere in the 1950s; and it used a mixture of steam locomotives and diesel cars on rural services more sensibly than any region of British Railways, the timetable skilfully producing a full-scale train at a peak time, with railcars, some stopping at level crossings as well as stations, filling in quieter periods. The company avoided needless centralization, leaving locomotives stabled overnight at many branch-line termini, and thus running a dense service of up trains in the morning and down trains in the evening without empty mileage against the traffic flow. Eight daily trains on the Great Northern usually provided a service far more geared to people's needs than the same number in Britain.

The Great Northern of course had problems, not the least being its seventeen different crossings of the border – mainly at rural points – between the two countries whose governments for years had no direct dealings, and which ironically were first brought together in the late 1950s to discuss the railway's demise. Customs formalities delayed passengers and freight alike. South of the border the railway controlled many of the bus services in its area and did so sensibly. North of it, politics decreed railways should not run buses; they ran in unfettered competition. Regulations for almost everything were different between North and South. Just what the management had to contend with in the 1920s as lifestyles diverged is shown by a scrapbook of instructions and notices to stationmasters.

Though much of the traffic was in fact suburban, the railway ever reflected the fact that Ireland is essentially rural, most townspeople having country or sporting pursuits. There are pages of regulations for the laying down of straw and other litter on the floor for different types of livestock – and 'All horned stock carried in the same railway truck with a bull shall, unless separated therefrom by a suitable partition, be securely tied by the head and the neck'; the Free State introduces control on transporting materials – including even golden syrup and brown sugar – that could be used for illicit distilling; rules for the conveyance of seed potatoes across the border become ever more complicated especially in years of scab. Racehorses are continually the subject of instructions: where a horse occupies more than one stall in a horsebox, it is regarded as going first class at a fare and a half; details for the working of race traffic run to many printed pages – 'The charges on horses from Stations within a 55 mile radius of Dublin will be paid by the Baldoyle Race Company'; the groom in charge of a racehorse has to affix a sixpenny stamp to the indemnity form on behalf of owner or trainer. And now cattle for breeding purposes are allowed to go at one and a half fares by goods or passenger train for the return journey – 'the same conditions as are applicable to Mares and Stallions'. Guinness empties are suddenly carried at much reduced price to combat road competition.

The general manager warns that the results for 1926 will be even worse than those for 1925: 'Much of our present difficulty is beyond the power of the staff to remove. The existing depression in trade may be a long one, and road motor competition, largely unfair in the present state of the Law, may yet become keener still; but every member of staff, especially those in positions of authority however small, can help the concern by trying to influence more traffic to the Line, by exercising the strictest economy, and by doing their utmost to make the Railway attractive to possible travellers and senders of goods.'

After 1939 Regulations became yet more complicated, for the line was now linking a country at war and one that remained neutral, albeit many men crossed the border to join up. Agricultural produce moved in larger quantities – in all kinds of ways, including on the racks of crowded local passenger trains taking northerners home after a foray into the more plentiful south. So the beginning of the final cash crisis was put off until 1950; and for several years more the system remained almost intact, down to the horse-drawn tram linking Fintona with the main line. But in 1958

An extract from the Great Northern's notice of special arrangements.

On same date an Engine and Van must run from Portadown to Dungannon and return to connect with the 8-45 a.m. Up Special ex Antrim as under : —

ENGINE AND VAN.				HORSES.				
			a.m.					a.m.
Portadown	..	.. dep.	8 30	Dungannon	..	..	dep.	9 42
Dungannon	..	.. arr.	8 55	Trew & Moy	..	..	arr.	9 50
				,,	..	..	dep.	9 55
				Portadown	..	..	arr.	10 10

The 9-45 a.m. Special to cross at Dungannon the 8-25 a.m. ex Belfast Loco to provide Engine and Portadown Agent Guard and Van

On same date, (Saturday, 31st July), a Special Train will run from Belfast (Maysfields) to Dublin working forward horses for the Show as under:—

					a.m.	
Belfast (Maysfields)	..	..	..	dep	9 40	
Central Jct.	..	..	..	pass	5..	Precede 9-45 a.m. Up Goods.
Lisburn	..	..	..	arr.	10 18	
,,	..	..	..	dep.	10 35	Follow 10-15 a.m. Up
Portadown	..	..	..	arr.	11 0	
,,	..	..	..	dep.	11 10	
Scarva	..	..	..	arr.	11 30	
,,	..	..	..	dep.	11 35	
Goraghwood	..	..	..	arr.	11 50	
,,	..	..	..	dep.	11 55	
Dundalk	..	..	..	arr.	12 35	
,,	..	..	..	dep.	12 45	
Castlebellingham	..	..	..	pass		Precede 4-0 a.m. Up Goods
Dromin	..	..	..	arr.	1 5	
,,	..	..	..	dep.	1 10	
Drogheda	..	..	..	arr.	1 40	} Check & Collect Grooms Tcts
,,	..	..	..	dep.	1 45	
Dublin	..	..	..	arr.	3 0	

Loco. to provide Engine and Control Dept. Van and Guard

As soon as the vehicles have been unloaded at the Show Siding and handed over to us at Amiens Street, they must be run Special to Belfast, stopping where necessary, to distribute Horse Boxes as may be advised by Plant Superintendent. Control Dept. to arrange for the return of the L.M. & S. Co.'s vehicles, which must be left off at Lisburn, and also any Co. Down Co's vehicles.

Horse Boxes, etc., for the Show Siding to be worked into the respective Junctions by the earlier trains so as to connect with this Special which on arrival at Amiens St., will be handed over to G. S. Co. for conveyance to Ballsbridge.

All Empty Horse Boxes not required for use in the Northern area, must be run special to Drogheda to be disinfected and held in readiness for the return traffic. Dublin Goods Agent to arrange to take over the boxes on arrival.

the rails were closed in a large part of the north-west, leaving Donegal, Tyrone, Fermanagh and Monaghan without trains and with a trail of hardship. In 1958 the Great Northern, by now the last line crossing the border, ceased to be, its truncated remains being divided between the nationalized systems of Ulster and Eire. The GN(I) was another railway fraught with troubles, but it had served its countryside well and demonstrated what so many people believed – that most of Britain's rural areas could have been better treated with less expense.

The brighter spots in the Irish picture highlight the general gloom. With the slow pace of road development and the general backwardness, here as much as anywhere in Europe what was needed was flexibility, maybe a combination of national ownership and local enterprise as the French have occasionally used successfully. Standardization in building and equipping would have helped; so would standard narrow-gauge locomotive classes, their major repairs concentrated at a central depot; but apart from their inevitable overheads, larger distant managements could not keep sufficiently in touch with local traffic potentials and pressures. Leasing lines under central control and inspection to small companies who could have thrown their total enthusiasm into daily management and traffic-finding would dramatically have improved margins. Involving local authorities was bound to prove disastrous, especially in Ireland.

Before we finally leave Ireland, for sheer enjoyment, a mention of one other narrow-gauge line, in many ways the most rural, the most memorable of them all, the last to run substantially beside a public road, a railway perpetually in the red, so criticized by the ratepayers that the press was afraid to report their meetings for fear of libel: the Tralee & Dingle. Forgetting its troublesome birth and the dozens of times it nearly died or killed its passengers, we will look at it long after passengers had been transferred to the now tarred road, even the ordinary goods trains had stopped, and all that remained were monthly cattle specials. Road transport could still not meet this peak demand in the early 1950s. So, a procession of two engines, seventeen cattle trucks and an ex-passenger brake van converted into half cattle wagon and half guard's van (the brake in the middle of the cattle section reached by stretching over a makeshift partition), and occasionally a second train, came to life. Patrick Whitehouse, a railway writer early enough on the scene to enjoy such institutions before they disappeared, called it the last piece of adventurous railroading to be found in the British Isles. He records how the empty stock never left Tralee on time on the Friday because the staff insisted on being paid first; how every effort was made to find enough ageing ex-Tralee & Dingle men, since other railwaymen would not do the job even if they were bribed; and how the fireman of the leading engine would climb on to the coal-bunker lid to pelt cattle and sheep grazing between the rails with briquettes to clear a passage for the train – none of George Stephenson's confidence that it would be 'the worse for the coo' here. We pick up Patrick Whitehouse at Castlegregory Junction.

All were expected to join Paddy in a good glass of porter at Fitzgerald's bar over the road, and never was a bar so well placed. Soon both safety-valves would lift in a deafening roar, for these little engines were never short of steam. Shortly the crew would return to begin the battle ... against nature, for the train stood at the foot of the celebrated Glenagalt Bank, certainly the most formidable in Ireland and probably unsurpassed in length and severity anywhere in the British Isles. The rails climbed from almost sea-level to a height of 680 feet in just under four miles, with ruling gradients of 1 in 30 and 1 in 31. It was bad enough when maintenance was good, but with the grass lying over the rails life became difficult in the extreme.

Not far from Castlegregory Junction was a steel bridge set upon a most acute semi-circular curve, close to the spot where once there was an even steeper grade and a more vicious curve, abandoned as the result of an accident when a mixed train from Dingle ran away from the summit and plunged from the rails into the gully fifty feet below. Drivers would never hesitate to point this out gleefully ...

From here the line twisted and turned following each indentation in the hillside and all the time descending in long stretches of 1 in 29–30. Footplate passengers glanced at the vacuum brake for reassurance, remembering the fitter back at Tralee tinkering with the hose coupling rubbers to cure the worst of the leakage. As the train came shaking down the hillside with the weatherbeaten cattle trucks wagging wildly there was still the sheep hazard to contend with and this was met by firm brake application, open drain-cocks and the squeal of flanges. The temporary panic over, then gravity once more took charge and the train bowled down the bank at 25–30 mph, the engines nosing their way along the rusty grass-grown track. One thought quickly of the four men employed to maintain these thirty-one miles of narrow-gauge track, and here again men and machines took refreshment, but alas the village bar was too far for a visit. But all was not lost, for here was yet another factotum sent down by the bus from Tralee for the weekend. He had the requisite bottles. The water point for engines lay beyond the station level crossing at the Dingle end of the yard, so by the time both engines had been watered and pleasantries exchanged, a minor traffic jam of lorries and donkey-carts was in evidence on the road. But this was of no importance ...

And so on to Dingle and the most westerly rails in Europe.

*

The Isle of Man, like several Mediterranean islands, showed how railways could rule life in a mini-kingdom where the average journey cannot have been more than a dozen miles. People went to school and work, shopped, attended meetings and sporting events, and often worshipped, according to the timetable. There were boat trains, mixed and goods trains, trains with through coaches for different destinations, branch connections. Douglas had an extensive goods yard for cattle, timber, hay and other farm items plus all goods (including coal) imported from England and Scotland. I recall two trucks of cattle placed at the end of an evening train to Port Erin as recently as 1958, when five or six engines might be seen shunting or taking water at Douglas. The parcels offices at stations like Port Erin were on mainland scale, while Douglas passenger terminus was a handsome affair with four canopied platforms, proper signalling,

The June 1951 cattle fair at Dingle was especially busy and the railway's total motive power and rolling stock were pressed into service. Ivo Peters was at Anascaul to photograph a rare crossing, No. 8 returning to Tralee with a first relief consignment of animals while Nos. 1 and 2 headed the regular Dingle-bound empties.

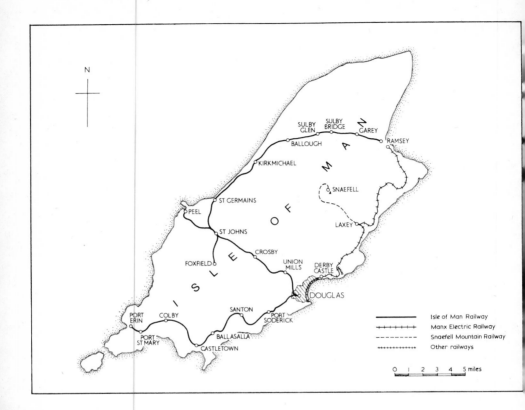

a truly Victorian booking hall, and a stone archway entrance which made you feel you were starting a journey of real importance. Out of that archway came a substantial proportion of the mainland's kipper supply for many years.

Even here there were the usual quarrels between promoters who at first thought they were about to make a fortune if their scheme could be pushed through and later had a weary struggle to finish the opening up of the island. Optimism sank fast; it is a far cry from the generosity of arrangements at Douglas on the Isle of Man Railway to the mean buildings on the Manx Northern Railway which took a roundabout west-coast route to Ramsey and suffered competition from the more direct east-coast electric tramway carrying the through mails.

158

Isle of Man pastoral, a Douglas train leaving St John's in June 1968.

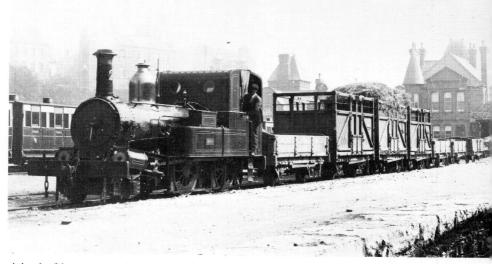

A load of hay among the goods in the yard at Douglas in about 1910.

A close-up of two of the island's well-kept locomotives, Nos. 4 and 13, crossing at a sylvan Ballasalla on the Port Erin line in July 1971.

The gauge was the same as Ireland's national narrow gauge, 3 feet, but otherwise the island railways followed British mainland practice and boasted of it. There was, however, one important cost-saving exception. Track maintenance was minimal, especially in relation to the weight and speed of trains hauled by the stud of well-kept 2-4-0 red tank locomotives. Long after buses run by the railway company reduced all-the-year-round services, holiday season trains carrying 300 and occasionally even 500 passengers (many using runabout tickets) seemed to glide through the grass at well over 40 miles an hour. Even the busiest section was worse maintained than British Railways goods-only branches used just two or three times a week. But not one passenger was killed; though high speed was for many years combined with lack of continuous brake. If British Railways could have trimmed their track costs the taxpayer would have been saved millions of pounds.

In the end the Isle of Man system became as anachronistic as any deliberately-preserved line. Its fascination lay in the continuity of use of its locomotives, rolling stock, stations, signalling, workshops (the system had always been totally self-sufficient) and everything else since the days when anyone going any distance in a hurry turned to the train. Much had been unaltered for exactly a century. Though a few half-hearted efforts were made to keep things going – a two-car diesel train was imported from the County Donegal when that closed – in the end only the Douglas–Port Erin route was retained for a subsidized 'Victorian Steam Railway' service; and currently only the Port Erin end of that line is in use.

10 The Railway in the Landscape

Railways were at once accepted in the landscape with a readiness that astonishes our present generation, driven by the multiplicity of incursions to oppose them all. Artists and engravers portrayed the lines lovingly, and writers of Murray's *Handbooks* assumed readers would want to be told where to view 'the wreaths of white smoke that float above the deep foliage' and how to reach great viaducts that could only be appreciated from the valley bottom rather than from the train. For the railways were the first great improver, welcomed and understood by all classes; and though with the enclosures the British landscape had just undergone its greatest transition, pressures from outside were minimal. So far as the canals had been noticed at all, they had added interest rather than spoilt the countryside. Then, the railways were built by men of taste to blend with the country they served; local materials were nearly always used in the early days, and nobody questioned the need for decorative touches such as gothic portals to tunnels.

Though there are much-quoted examples of tunnels having to be built solely to hide the trains, and for over forty years the Midland Railway's route from Leicester to Peterborough had to skirt awkwardly round Stapleford Park at Saxby, until a new landowner allowed a realignment, generally speaking even the wealthy landowners who had thrown fits of opposition were merely after the best compensation terms. They usually stayed on their estates to enjoy both the cash and the trains. As we have seen, the armies of navvies were frightening enough, but what they left behind was quickly absorbed and liked, the sheer scale often inspiring awe, the continuity contrasting nicely with the patchwork of farms and fields. Only in mountainous areas, notably the Lake District, where the railway endangered the scale, was there real opposition on aesthetic grounds.

162

'Nobody questioned the need for decorative touches.'

Local pride was often intense, guide books extolling the architectural features and convenience of even the badly built stations and welcoming the trains even when they cut off a sea view or split a place in two. Cullen on the Banffshire coast was crudely divided, the railway arch narrowing the main street by more than half; but by the time people realized its inconvenience the arch had become a local feature, and though no trains have crossed it for years and it hampers road traffic, its demolition is bitterly resisted.

The railways were liked – by virtually everyone. Archaeologists welcomed the opportunities for discoveries of fossils and Roman remains, and perhaps even more the public interest these discoveries aroused. Geologists excitedly studied rock faults laid bare by tunnels and embankments. Naturalists noted how different vegetation grew on new ground and quickly appreciated that a 300-ton train disturbed wildlife less than a man on foot. Above all, the railways brought a new realization of the beauty and variety of the British Isles. Encouraged by Queen Victoria's travels – from the start she was an ardent enthusiast for railways – and by paintings and photographs from the companies' emerging publicity departments, people began looking at their surroundings with new eyes, planning train itineraries, taking window seats armed with guides

163

On this and the opposite page are three early artists' impressions of the country railway. Published by Day and Hughe, lithographers to the king, the first shows an improbably romantic scene, even the livestock have decoratively arranged themselves. The other two are by unknown artists, the top being a photograph of a painting (note the man carrying a load over his shoulder as he leads two passengers to wait for the approaching train) and the lower shows Ealing's then village station in 1839.

which of course assumed rail travel, and comparing the scenic rating of rival routes.

The Midland never offered the quickest way to Scotland, but many chose it because it was the pleasantest, with breathtaking scenery north of Leeds. This Waverley route on across the high moors of the border country to Edinburgh became an international institution. Holiday journeys were timed to see the spectacular parts in daylight, advice always being readily given on the best side to sit, the loveliest stretches of moorland, river and coast. And at its height the railway system commanded a remarkable range of all three.

The railways popularized the country as well as opening it up. Hundreds of thousands of slum dwellers who may have missed out on the finer points of hill and valley scenery none the less sooner or later breathed country air and found some new dimension to life. There were

165

Sunday-school and works outings, charity excursions for poor and disabled children, harvest and hop pickers' specials – and 'friends' specials' to visit the hop pickers in the middle of their ritual stint. Up to 100,000 'friends' a season were carried from London to Kent stations alone over half a century ended by the second world war, though the 'hoppers' only finally faded with the advent of holidays with pay (and mechanical picking) in the mid-1950s.

Until then railwaymen along with most other workers could only go on holiday by forfeiting wages and – except for crews in the course of duty – rarely packed their bags. But they might explore the greater part of Britain on day trips. Excursions often travelled incredible distances at a fraction of an old penny a mile, with especially generous programmes from the main centres of population served by rival routes. From around the turn of the century, for little more than a week's wages an averagely paid Birmingham skilled worker might visit Yarmouth, Weston-super-Mare, Llandrindod Wells, Morecambe and Grassington in a single season. Day excursions often meant spending part of two nights in the train; Glaswegians could thus reach England's south coast.

Inland destinations were relatively more popular and many a place now in a National Park had its greatest influx of visitors before the war. Up to 50 full-length excursion trains reached Lake District stations at high-summer weekends. On Sundays and bank holidays, Sheffield and Leeds were typical North Country cities sending thousands to moorland stations. Before stately homes opened their doors to visitors, trains disgorged thousands to walk round Tintern and Bolton Abbeys and the Welsh castles. Some excursions included cycle vans; walkers' tickets out to one station and back from another were popular for two generations. Excursion trains arriving at small towns tended to have the same effect as modern cruise liners' calls at 'unspoilt' Pacific islands, but every country station received a modest quota of discerning hikers and sightseers. Doing a village involved getting preliminary advice from the porter collecting the outward half of the ticket, walking to the centre and count-

The West Coast route to Scotland in the Lune Gorge with a class 5 locomotive on an up train seen from Grayrigg Pike in August 1957. The coming of the motorway did far more visual damage than the railway.

166

ing the shops and wondering when their window displays had last been changed, looking at the church and its monuments, buying a penny bun, strolling back early to the station to be invited into the office to share warmth and gossip.

It was round the same fire that in later years local people who now normally drove into the nearest town to work or shop clustered on snowy mornings when the road was impassable and the train – though running – was probably late. The furniture and pictures were perhaps the same as when these people caught the same train to school each morning, years ago. But now the parcels section was emptier; the odd bicycle resting in the corner belonged to a child who was collected by car from boarding-school at term's end; that parcel contained a spare part for a machine delivered by lorry. The railway was down to carrying odds and ends, seen as an insurance policy and convenience rather than a basic essential. But even when the service had been halved, not by producing a balanced skeleton timetable but by cutting out half the trains and leaving impossible gaps, when stations were left unpainted, their gardens overgrown, threat of closure brought spontaneous, united opposition.

Even the occasional closure in the nineteenth century had been unpopular; once a railway, always a railway, as envisaged in the 'in perpetuity' clauses in many Acts. Most closures in the first half of this century took the guise of temporary war economy or fuel saving. But from 1950 they were as common as openings had been a century earlier, and evolved their own setpiece rituals.

'The continuity contrasting nicely with the patchwork of farms and fields.' An Ivatt 2-6-2T and standard 2-6-4T make light work of a northbound local on the Somerset & Dorset, crossing Prestleigh Viaduct near Shepton Mallet.

The railways presented the case for closure to the regional Transport Users' Consultative Committee, the procedures being detailed in posters inspiringly headed 'Public notice'. If there were objectors – there invariably were, local authorities arguing with standardized ferocity irrespective of individual circumstance – an enquiry would be held. This was usually something of a farce, objectors astonishingly not being allowed to query British Railways' facts and figures, though to say the least these were often of questionable accuracy, and nobody could tell what central overheads had been charged to the branch or whether any credit had been given for through traffic starting on it.[1] The submissions did however show how wasteful management had been, how on many lines of 20 or so miles £25,000 a year could have been saved over the previous decade through reasonable economies such as simplified signalling and leaving the guard to issue tickets. However difficult it might be to make the railways pay their way now, much of the loss piled up in the 1950s and 1960s could have been avoided; but whereas pay trains, on which the guard collects fares, serve substantial towns today, in 1960 the largest region, the London Midland, was even opposed to having any unstaffed halt – where trains called at all, they had to be met by at least a porter. And while there is now only a single track between Salisbury and Exeter, where the *Atlantic Coast Express* once raced in three or four portions in peak summer, earlier nobody was interested in singling cross-country links carrying mere handfuls of passengers.

The regional committee had to judge what hardship (as opposed to mere inconvenience) might be caused, and how effective the replacement buses would be. Rarely did it suggest the trains should be retained, and when it did the judgement was often overturned by the Central Transport Users' Consultative Committee vetting the work of the regional ones; and anyway the final say was with a Minister of Transport committed to retrenchment. Yet where passenger trains were withdrawn, goods usually continued for several years more, gangers and even signalmen

1. For their part railway officials sometimes found annoyingly large numbers of passengers in the annual census returns of stations under threat. The stationmaster or porter would drop a hint of the dates the count was to be taken and supporters would make trips and encourage friends to break their journey. But then for generations the dates of visits by judges of Best Kept Station competitions had been leaked and passengers often helped improve displays perhaps with temporarily loaned plants and flowers.

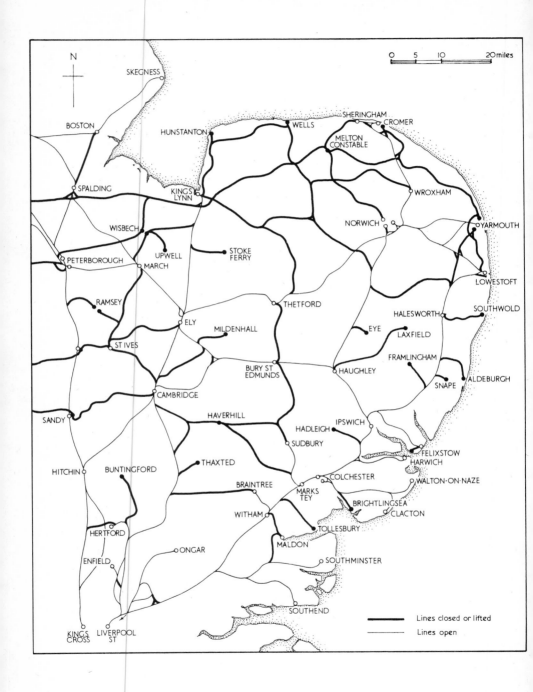

N

SKEGNESS

BOSTON

SPALDING

HUNSTANTON

WELLS

SHERINGHAM
CROMER

MELTON
CONSTABLE

WROXHAM

KINGS
LYNN

WISBECH

NORWICH

YARMOUTH

PETERBOROUGH

UPWELL

STOKE
FERRY

MARCH

LOWESTOFT

RAMSEY

THETFORD

HALESWORTH

SOUTHWOLD

ELY

MILDENHALL

EYE

LAXFIELD

ST IVES

FRAMLINGHAM

BURY ST
EDMUNDS

HAUGHLEY

SNAPE

ALDEBURGH

CAMBRIDGE

SANDY

HAVERHILL

IPSWICH

HADLEIGH

FELIXSTOW

HITCHIN

BUNTINGFORD

THAXTED

SUDBURY

HARWICH

WALTON·ON·NAZE

BRAINTREE

COLCHESTER

MARKS
TEY

BRIGHTLINGSEA

HERTFORD

WITHAM

CLACTON

ENFIELD

ONGAR

TOLLESBURY

MALDON

SOUTHMINSTER

KINGS
CROSS

LIVERPOOL
ST

SOUTHEND

0   5   10   20 miles

Lines closed or lifted

Lines open

remaining on the job. The replacement buses, even when subsidized, rarely connected with main-line trains. Usually less than one in three ex-railway passengers transferred to them. Many families were forced or preferred to buy cars, change jobs or move. Village taxi services succumbed along with railway pubs.

Of course money had to be saved, and of course in the end most branch lines would have had to close, but it was all unnecessarily harsh and wasteful, making a mockery of rural planning. And no one but the railways themselves was surprised to discover that when branches closed people did not always faithfully catch the train from the nearest remaining railhead, and that lopping many thousands of miles off the system failed to reduce central overheads.

After months of frustration, the actual closure came as a relief, an occasion for uninhibited demonstration of a kind only equalled by the celebrations of the jubilee, coronations and two peaces since the valley welcomed its first train. Those who had not patronized the line for years were overcome with nostalgia for times they imagined had once been, and were taken aback by the view from a viaduct or the lush verdure of the cuttings. Helped by bands of enthusiasts who went from burial to burial, each community did its best to stamp the passing of the railway age on the memories of the young. The detonators and wreaths, a competition to buy the last ticket, much of the gossip – 'what a beautiful way to see the countryside' – were much the same from Helston in Cornwall, where we began, to Northumberland, and from Pembrokeshire to the Moray coast, though of course local colour also shone through. Country people enjoy an occasion; in Ireland so much that it was often felt prudent quietly to change over to buses several days ahead of the expected date.

The railway map contracted far more rapidly than was sensible or practical without widespread disruption and hardship, more suddenly than in most civilized countries facing the same problems. One keeps saying that if only economies had started earlier and a handful of busier lines

This up-to-date map marks lines closed to passengers more boldly than the smaller number remaining open: it demonstrates the extent of losses in East Anglia. Norfolk has suffered especially severely, closures including virtually all the cross-country Midland & Great Northern system from the Midlands to Yarmouth.

171

Perhaps the most spectacular scenery still to be seen from a British train is on
the West Highland route to Mallaig. Opposite, a Fort William train is
dwarfed by the mountain as it approaches Glenfinnan. Above, a Mallaig train
crosses Glenfinnan Viaduct. Below, a Glasgow train near Lochailort.

closed in the 1960s were still at work today, how much everyone including the taxpayer would have gained; one is still amazed by that figure already quoted: over a thousand *steam* locomotives built by British Railways after nationalization. Nor is this criticism mere hindsight; many experts called for positive, constructive economy such as the greater use of diesel railcars from the late 1940s onward. As seen in the chapter on the country train, when the diesels did belatedly arrive, new, clean, not the traditional left-overs from busier routes, they drastically cut costs and attracted a new generation of scenery lovers; for the first time you could see the railway in the landscape from the train itself, especially welcome on mountainous cross-country lines as between Barnard Castle and Penrith.

All is not gone. Even in my West Country, you can still sit behind the driver sharing his outlook on your way to Barnstaple, Gunnislake, Looe, St Ives, all memorable journeys. The railways still pass through some of Britain's best scenery, over two fine highlands even on the inter-city electrified route from Euston to Glasgow, along the cliffs on that from King's Cross to Edinburgh and again on to Aberdeen; they cross and hug estuaries, play hide and seek with many a river; they will still drop you or pick you up at hundreds of country stations, many with hardly a house in sight, and treat you to their own interpretations of the Broads and Fens; they still carry you the length of Central Wales, and here and there, where the train has a special role and advantage over road transport, still let you mix with people going to market.

The heritage is increasingly valued. There is for instance a greater

A Pwllheli diesel multiple-unit train allegedly costing the taxpayer several pounds a mile, but still much valued, descends the bank into Fairbourne on the Cambrian coastline.

Dent, the highest main-line station in England, on the Midland's route to Scotland, as it was in steam days before closure, and below passengers alighting from a Dales Rail train in 1975.

demand for booklets describing key routes now than since the 1930s. Just as Americans are rediscovering the joys of train travel in their own country, more come to Britain to explore it by rail, planning itineraries carefully, anxious not to miss a glimpse of picturesque village or ancient cathedral. Many of the steam lines run privately will survive not through people playing trains but because young and old come to enjoy the scenery they unlock, reaching places inaccessible by road or with inadequate parking facilities, winding along shelves cut into the mountain sides, jumping over ravines, intimately immersed in their landscape.

Opposition to further closures, such as that of the section from Dovey Junction through Barmouth to Pwllheli, 53 miles hugging the Welsh coast and offering a perspective totally different from the road's, is better-informed and more likely to succeed. The railway is now seen as a valuable part of the environment. Frequently local opinion is forcing management into action; would British Railways still be running their only steam and narrow-gauge line up the Rheidol Valley to Devil's Bridge but for the success of the early volunteer-operated systems? Local authorities, too, begin to come in with practical help, looking after station gardens, paying for facelifts to buildings or the reopening of stations, such as several in the Fens. Organizations such as the National Trust increasingly include trains in their programmes; the railway is part of our country heritage.

Perhaps the most interesting experiment to date is the Dales Rail, organized by the Dales National Park Committee, Cumbria County and Eden District Councils, and the Countryside Commission. In 1975 a number of intermediate stations on the Settle & Carlisle section of the former Midland route to Scotland were reopened for occasional weekend trains, taking walkers out into the country, and country people into the city to shop. Not only was it popular, it actually paid its way. A slightly more ambitious programme in 1976 connected the trains and special buses with 17 guided walks, many of them starting at one point and finishing at another – the one thing that the near-supreme flexibility of the private car does not allow. Schedules, fares and publicity are imaginative, and though inflation ever threatens schemes supported out of public funds, it looks as though passengers of many types will use reopened Dent, the highest main-line station in England, for as long as the route remains open.

176

'*Every full moon it comes belting through – and the funny thing is it seems to do our cabbages a power o' good.*'

Even abandoned routes – already over 6,000 miles of them in Britain – are part of the country heritage. A few have been turned into walks: the Tissington Trail takes in the Buxton–Ashbourne line, the Wirral Way in Cheshire is focused on the Hooton–West Kirby section, and a mile of that very rural concern the Glyn Valley Tramway near Glynceiriog is an attractive riverside path belonging to the National Trust. More such conversions are on the way; such schemes have sometimes been opposed by farmers fearful for crops and livestock, though experience gained on the continuous coastal footpaths should be reassuring. It does not however require a formal footpath to attract walkers, explorers and wildlife lovers to old railways. Following an abandoned line gives point to an afternoon's expedition; a cutting may yield blackberries, or a deserted Scottish station wild raspberries; primrose, cowslip and meadow cranesbill flourish undisturbed as in few other locations. Some of the best unofficial nature reserves have long been those thickets occupying small pockets of land beside a river where the railway temporarily deserts the bank to take a straighter course. As an instance of changing times, Richard Mabey points out in *The Roadside Wildlife Book* that the ending of steam stopped the migration of West Country ferns, whose spores rode the rods east and settled in the stonework of north-facing bridges and platforms, kept damp by the steam; but there are ever new influences at work.

An imaginative current enterprise is to be found on the south-eastern outskirts of Doncaster. The remains of a once-vast area of pure reed fen, the 250-acre Potteric Carr, is owned by British Railways, several of whose routes (including the main East Coast line to Scotland) pass or cross it. Though officials were at first nonplussed at naturalists' enthusiasm for the soggy waste, in 1968 the County Trust began leasing it, and now signalmen act as unofficial gamekeepers, reporting poachers. Several rare species flourish here, and the reserve's management committee's substantial annual report shows just how much hard work is needed to protect them. The foreword is by the railway divisional manager who points out

One track has already been removed and vegetation begins to move in. Even though this is a crowded island, the cutting will probably remain an unofficial nature reserve for centuries to come. Ivatt 2-6-0 No. 43049 coasts into Kirkby Stephen East.

The East Coast main line beside Low Ellers marsh of Potterick Carr.

the environmental advantages of rail travel, explains that realignment of
the East Coast route to take high-speed trains will place strains on Potterick Carr, and offers full co-operation in preserving the essential marsh.

Only the revolution in basic agriculture had a greater influence on the
landscape than did the railways. Whether or not trains still run, much
of the work of the navvies will be seen and explored as long as civilization
lasts. We are only beginning to appreciate the potential of the almost endless wildlife reserves where even after a generation or two – medick often
being the first plant to colonize the ballast, others rooting in its yellow
carpet, adjoining woodlands regenerating – there are likely to be more
species of plants and birds than in typical roadside hedges.

180

Appendix: The Abermule Disaster

The following is an extract from L. T. C. Rolt's Red For Danger *(see pages 105–6)*

The story of the events which resulted in the Abermule disaster is a classic example of the truth that no electrical or mechanical safety devices can altogether eliminate the human element: that the safety of the travelling public must always depend, in the last analysis, upon the efficiency and vigilance of the railway staff. The 10.5 am stopping train from Whitchurch was scheduled to cross the Aberystwyth to Manchester express shortly before noon at Abermule, a small country station in the valley of the upper Severn and the junction for the short Kerry branch. But this arrangement was not rigidly enforced. If either train happened to be behind time then they might pass each other at the next station to the north or south of Abermule. If the stopping train was late it might be held for the express at Montgomery but if it was running to time and the express was delayed, then Abermule might send it on to Newtown. On this January day the staff at Abermule station was as follows: relief Stationmaster Lewis, deputizing for the regular stationmaster who was on leave; Signalman Jones; a youthful porter named Rodgers and a boy named Francis Thompson who collected tickets and helped in the booking office. It is important to remember these four for although they remained remote from the actual scene of the accident they were the chief actors in the drama. For the tragedy was entirely due to their combined carelessness added to the fact that there was no proper co-ordination at the station in the carrying out of their respective duties. In the light of this lack of proper organization, the fact that the Tyer electric tablet instruments were installed in the station building and not in the signal cabin was most unfortunate. Only the stationmaster and the signalman, Jones, were supposed to work the tablet instruments, but it had become the practice for anyone to work them who happened to be handy.

When Montgomery advised Abermule at 11.50 am that the stopping train had arrived there and was waiting to proceed it was Signalman Jones who replied. He was in the instrument room with Rodgers and Thompson. Stationmaster Lewis had gone for his dinner. Jones accepted the train and pressed the release on the Montgomery–Abermule instrument which enabled his mate at Montgomery to withdraw the necessary tablet. Having done so he rang up Moat Lane Junction, the next station south of Newtown, to ask the whereabouts of the express. Moat Lane replied that it had left there and was on its way to Newtown. Having received this information, the signalman left the instrument room and went along to his cabin at the end of the platform to set the road and open the level crossing gates for the stopping train. On his way out he met the returning stationmaster but he did not say anything to him about the position of the two approaching trains. Lewis did not stay in the instrument room but went off to the goods yard to superintend the movement of some wagons, leaving the young porter, Rodgers, and the boy Thompson in charge. At this juncture Newtown rang up saying that the express had arrived there and asking permission to send it forward. This time it was Rodgers who accepted the train and pressed the release on the Abermule–Newtown instrument which enabled Newtown to withdraw a tablet. So far, everything was in order; the two trains were approaching Abermule from opposite directions, each bearing the correct tablet for the section it occupied while both the tablet instruments at Abermule were now automatically locked so that no other tablet could be withdrawn. Rodgers now left the instrument room and went to the ground frame at the opposite end of the platform from the signal cabin with the object of setting the road for the express to enter the passing loop. Lewis the station-master was still in the goods yard so the youth did not tell him that he had accepted the express. The ground frame levers were locked from the cabin. Had Rodgers called on Signalman Jones to release the lock, the latter would have realized that the express was approaching, but at this moment Rodgers was diverted from his intention by the arrival of the stopping train from Mont-gomery. Jones knew from his telephone inquiry to Moat Lane that the express was running to time, but only Rodgers knew positively that the express was actually occupying the Newtown–Abermule section and even having regard to his youth his subsequent inaction is hard to explain. The boy Thompson was beside him when he accepted the express but evidently he did not realize what Rodgers had done. Thompson was alone on the up platform when the stopping train ran in on the down side. He immediately crossed the line and collected the Montgomery–Abermule tablet from the driver. He climbed back on to the up platform with the intention of returning the tablet to the instrument when he met the stationmaster hurrying up from the goods yard. Lewis asked Thompson where the express was and the boy inexplicably replied that it had just passed Moat Lane, thus giving Lewis the false impression that it was running late. As he gave this misleading information the boy made another terrible mistake; without any explanation he handed the Montgomery–Abermule tablet he had just collected to the stationmaster with the remark that he must go to the station exit to take the tickets. Now it was Lewis's turn to make confusion worse confounded. He had not been on the platform to observe the boy's actions and he assumed that Thompson had already replaced the Montgomery–Abermule tablet and, since he understood that the express was behind time, that the tablet he now held in his hand authorized the train in the station to proceed towards Newtown. In fact it would have been impossible to obtain such a tablet for the Abermule–Newtown instrument was locked. Had Lewis looked at the inscription on the tablet he would have seen that it was the wrong one, but he took it for granted that the boy had changed it, crossed the line and handed it back to the driver. Under working rules it was the driver's duty to examine the tablet and so ensure that it was correct, but he failed to do so. Like the stationmaster he took it for granted. For years the Tyer electric block system had protected the line infallibly and he conceived no possibility of error. Without troubling to remove it from its pouch, the driver placed it in his cab. It was his death warrant. Both the boy Thompson, who had returned from his ticket collecting, and Signalman Jones saw Lewis hand over the deadly tablet, but neither saw any reason to intervene. Thompson assumed that the stationmaster had changed the tablet in his absence. Jones, knowing the express was running to time, was surprised, but he too took for granted the infallibility of the system and assumed that for some reason unknown to him the express had been held at Newtown. Presumably Rodgers thought likewise and imagined that Newtown's request for acceptance had been cancelled and that the tablet whose release he had authorized had been replaced in the Newtown instrument. The road was accordingly set for the train to proceed towards Newtown, the signals were pulled off and the train went on its way. Only when it was too late did the Abermule staff discover that the Montgomery–Abermule instrument had not been cleared by the return of the tablet and so realized their terrible mistake.

The crew on the express locomotive miraculously escaped death and were afterwards able to give an account of the collision. They were travelling fast on a falling gradient about a mile from Abermule when, to their horror, they sighted the engine of the stopping train coming towards them at close range through a shallow cutting and labouring hard on the up-grade. Driver Pritchard Jones at once made a full emergency brake application, but to pull up his heavy train in time was quite impossible. Moreover, the crew of the oncoming train did not appear to see them for the locomotive continued to belch steam and smoke until the moment of impact. In that terrific collision the engine of the stopping train was overwhelmed and irreparably damaged by the heavier locomotive of the express, both enginemen being killed instantly. The framing of the express engine reared itself on end while the boiler was torn clean out of the frame and twisted through 180 degrees. The coaches of the slow-moving 'local' and the rear coaches of the express remained on the rails and were little damaged, but the leading express coaches were telescoped and wrecked. In them, fifteen passengers were killed including Lord Herbert Vane-Tempest, a Director of the Cambrian Railway Company. The wreckage was so inextricably locked together that it took the breakdown gang over fifty hours of continuous work to clear the line.

Although he was lying seriously injured under a pile of wreckage, Driver Pritchard Jones's first thought was to discover the cause of the accident. He had examined his tablet before leaving Newtown and found it was correct. Could he possibly have been mistaken? In desperate anxiety he called to his Fireman, Owen, and although the latter had also been injured he began frantically to search among the twisted wreckage of the two locomotives for the tablet. He eventually managed to recover two tablets: one was their own and correct, but the other was for the Montgomery–Abermule section and at once the presence of the stopping train was explained. Mr George, the Cambrian's Chief Traffic Inspector, who had been a passenger on the express, took both tablets from Owen and ran with them to Abermule station. The fatal tablet now became an instrument of mercy. In the presence of witnesses, George placed it in the Abermule–Montgomery machine, an action which cleared that section and allowed the breakdown train from Oswestry to proceed.

After commenting upon the mistakes and breaches of working rules at Abermule which had led up to the disaster, the inspecting officer, Colonel Pringle, went on to make certain recommendations which, he said, would prevent any recurrence. The fact that the tablet instruments were installed in the station building was a practice inherited, no doubt, from the old telegraph offices which the new system had replaced. The Colonel condemned it. The instruments should be in the signal cabin under the control of the signalman. No such misunderstanding could then occur. He also suggested that the tablet instruments should be interlocked with starting signals so that a starter could not be pulled off unless the relevant instrument had been cleared. Finally he criticized the layout at Abermule. Although it was locked from the box, the use of a separate and remote ground frame for controlling movements on running lines was objectionable .. . . .

For anyone connected with railways the name of this quiet little country station in the Welsh border country will always carry sinister and tragic overtones. The story of the apparently trivial events which defeated the most ingenious mechanical devices and so led to this appalling disaster has not staled with the passing of the years. On the contrary it still teaches so salutary a lesson that it should be compulsory reading for every newcomer to the railway service in any capacity. For at Abermule the locomotive crew of the stopping train and each member of the station staff from stationmaster to ticket boy contributed to the tragedy by their slackness and irresponsibility, by breaches of rule and by relying too much upon the infallibility of a mechanical system. We may take it as certain that the errors committed on this occasion were by no means unique. Not only at Abermule but at many another single line crossing station unauthorized staff had worked the tablet instruments or had passed tablets from hand to hand. Many another stationmaster had, for one reason or another, failed to be present on the arrival of a train and then authorized the 'right away' without proper assurance that all was as it should be. Many another driver had received a tablet without examining it. Time and again one or other of these mistakes had been made with impunity, but at Abermule on that disastrous day, like the scattered pieces of a jigsaw puzzle, these trifling faults fitted one into another until the sombre picture was complete.

Bibliography & Acknowledgements

This has been a fun book to write since at one time or another I have lived and breathed much of the material, both on the ground out in the countryside and in research for other writings. Touches of information have come from many past and present railwaymen and from all kinds of manuscript sources as well as from published transport history. A full bibliography would be lengthy and pointless. I am therefore limiting the scope to titles of general interest which those who have enjoyed this book might read and to histories of a few of the individual railways that figure in these pages.

Two outstanding general railway histories are Jack Simmons: *The Railways of Britain* (1961) and Michael Robbins: *The Railway Age* (1962). Terry Coleman: *The Railway Navvies* (1965), Gordon Biddle: *Victorian Stations* (1973) and L. T. C. Rolt: *Red For Danger* (1955) are key titles on important aspects. Of more specific rural interest are W. J. K. Davies: *Light Railways* (1964) and P. B. Whitehouse: *On the Narrow Gauge* (1964), while my own *The Rural Transport Problem* (1963) deals with sociological aspects. Ernest J. Simmons: *Memoirs of a Station Master*, edited by Jack Simmons (1974) captures the atmosphere among the staff at country stations in Victoria's reign. Christabel S. Orwin and Edith H. Whetham: *History of British Agriculture 1846–1914* (1964, 1971) is perhaps the most useful general history of life and times on the land. Several titles of country reminiscences have been mentioned in the text but no single one has sufficient railway information to warrant listing here. Much of Richard Mabey: *The Roadside Wildlife Book* (1974) has equal relevance to railways.

Reasonably detailed accounts of regional development against the social and economic background are included in the volumes of the expanding 'A Regional History of the Railways of Great Britain' series, while abandoned systems are lovingly portrayed in the complementary 'Forgotten Railways' series, and Ireland is served by H. C. Casserley: *Outline of Irish Railway History* (1974). Individual railway histories on lines mentioned in this book include Robin Atthill: *The Somerset & Dorset Railway* (1967), Peter E. Baughan: *The Railways of*

186

Wharfedale (1969), J. I. C. Boyd: *The Isle of Man Railway* (1962), Rex Christiansen and R. W. Miller: *The Cambrian Railways* (two volumes, 1967, 1969), A. T. Newham: *The Schull & Skibbereen Tramway* (booklet, 1964), Edward M. Patterson: *The County Donegal Railways* (1962), N. J. Stapleton: *The Kelvedon & Tollesbury Light Railway* (booklet, 1962) and John Thomas: *The West Highland Railway* (1965). Several of these writers are among those who have also given individual assistance with material for this book, but it would be impossible to list the many people who have helped in one way or another and so a general thanks must suffice: one just could not undertake a task like this, touching on a large number of different subjects, without a helpful circle of colleagues and friends. In the office Geoffrey Kichenside has helped trace illustrations, and my namesake and good friend John Thomas also gave much help. Mrs Miriam Stone and Miss Linda Skinner typed the manuscript, and my wife Pamela has as usual helped keep me on the rails. We have all enjoyed it and I hope it shows, as in the cartoons and drawings by Dennis Mallet. Maps are by Vic Welch. Many of the photographs come from my own collection and that of Locomotive & General Railway Photographs owned by David & Charles; others are acknowledged with thanks on page 6.

Index